Praise for
Flying Over the Pigpen

"Too many of today's management books are used to espouse the 'latest and greatest' buzzwords of management. The one sentiment that is rarely expressed and perhaps completely forgotten is a simple 'Thank you!' With *Flying Over the Pigpen*, we are invited along on a very personal journey that reflects the author's great appreciation for all of the people and life lessons that have allowed him to be successful. He skips the buzzwords and speaks directly from his heart. It is wonderfully refreshing!"

—Tom Moran
Chairman and CEO, Mutual of America

"From farm boy to turning around an organization on the brink of financial troubles to successfully leading a world-class organization, Tieman offers a high-level perspective on establishing a meaningful career. His detailed focus on accountability, high standards, positive and decisive leadership, and a passionate approach offers concrete lessons that help focus the mind on how to achieve successful and regularly improving outcomes. This highly readable book brings us deep inside a values-driven thinking process and thoughtful analysis that comfortably enlightens us on how to achieve long-term sustainable success for ourselves and the people in our organizations while benefiting the greater good."

—Ed Satell
Founder and CEO, Progressive Business Publications

"Great leaders know that they cannot do it alone. A critical component of leadership is not only doing your best but also bringing out the best in others through open, honest communication and collaboration.

"Doug Tieman's inspiring life story and decades of successful service in the not-for-profit sector provide all of us with valuable lessons and tools to make ourselves and those around us the best we can be. By bringing out the best in their teams, leaders bring out the best in themselves. The exponential impact of this collaboration emboldens leaders to 'promise the moon and deliver'!"

—**Daniel Hilferty**
President and CEO,
Independence Blue Cross

"Doug Tieman's record of leadership at the helm of the Richard Caron Foundation is impressive; how wonderful that he has compiled this amusing and useful 'down home' primer."

—**D. A. Donahue**
Partner, financial services firm

FLYING OVER THE PIGPEN

Leadership Lessons from Growing Up on a Farm

DOUG TIEMAN

Foreword by Christopher Kennedy Lawford

Health Communications, Inc.
Deerfield Beach, Florida

www.hcibooks.com

Library of Congress Cataloging-in-Publication Data
is available through the Library of Congress

© 2015 Doug Tieman

ISBN-13: 978-07573-1860-3 (Paperback)
ISBN-10: 07573-1860-6 (Paperback)
ISBN-13: 978-07573-1861-0 (ePub)
ISBN-10: 07573-1861-4 (ePub)

Publisher: Health Communications, Inc.
          3201 S.W. 15th Street
          Deerfield Beach, FL 33442–8190

Cover design by Larissa Hise Henoch
Interior design and formatting by Lawna Patterson Oldfield

*This book is dedicated
to my father, Leroy Tieman,
who gave me the foundation
for the life lessons
contained within.*

CONTENTS

Part 3: **ACT LIKE IT**

Part 4: **BE SUCCESSFUL**

Part 5: **WHAT NOW?**
ON TO THE NEXT LEVEL

Part 6: **CONCLUSION**

APPENDICES

FOREWORD

Doug Tieman understood at an early age that promising more than what is expected and delivering on those promises are the key ingredients to success. "Promise the moon and deliver" has been a mantra for Tieman since his childhood.

In the 1960s he joined a nation entranced with my uncle, President John F. Kennedy, and his proclamation that the United States would commit itself to landing an astronaut on the moon and returning him safely home. Less than a decade after those words were spoken, Tieman watched in awe as Neil Armstrong took the first human steps onto the moon. While Tieman's admiration for the astronaut was great, his admiration for the president who had announced the mission was even greater.

The fact that President Kennedy was able to motivate an entire nation to embrace and race toward the goal he had issued was not lost on Tieman. Even though the president did not live to witness the moon landing, he had delivered on his promise, and Tieman was determined to follow in his footsteps.

Inspired by a president and guided by a wise, hands-on father, Tieman learned to think big, work hard, and overachieve. He has been promising and delivering the moon his whole life, and inspiring others throughout his career to do the same.

A Living Legend at Caron Treatment Centers

Doug Tieman is a living legend at Caron Treatment Centers, where he has been president and CEO since 1995. Credited with leading the center to its current standing as a world-class facility, Tieman is revered for his ability to motivate management and employees, his immense energy for cultivating donors and fund-raising, and the drive and vision that place him among the top leaders of the addiction treatment industry.

After twenty years with Tieman at its helm, Caron enjoys annual revenues of more than $100 million. It operates residential treatment facilities in Pennsylvania and Florida and has regional offices in major cities along the East Coast that provide a range of services for alumni, patients, and families.

Caron continues its commitment to charity care by offering approximately $17 million in treatment scholarships every year.

A Challenge Results in Personal Triumph

Tieman has also dealt with personal challenges during his tenure as the CEO of Caron. In 2008, he was arrested and charged with driving while impaired. The arrest came just hours after Tieman presided over a packed fundraiser that brought in more than a million dollars.

Faced with his own addiction, Tieman did what he always does. He took responsibility and dedicated himself to growing, learning, and evolving.

Tieman immediately sought residential treatment at another well-respected facility and began his personal journey of recovery. He was subsequently reaffirmed by the Caron Board of Directors as President and CEO and welcomed back to work.

His experience offered him a renewed perspective regarding the possibilities and blessings of recovery. He remains committed to his personal recovery and to helping more individuals and their families access treatment.

The Heart of the Caron Story

While Tieman is at the center of Caron's remarkable success story, he is quick to share the credit with not only the board and his management team but also with every Caron employee.

Some may wonder why Tieman chose to join Caron twenty years ago when it was in the midst of a serious financial challenge. Tieman says it can be summarized in one word: heart. "I was so impressed with the dedication, expertise, compassion, and commitment to Caron's simple mantra of loving its patients back to health. I knew this is where I was meant to be," Tieman said. "Money can buy a lot of things, but it cannot buy heart."

With the heart of Caron firmly in the right place and Tieman at the helm of the organization, Caron will continue to give individuals and their families a second chance at life.

—Christopher Kennedy Lawford

PREFACE

When my brothers and I were growing up on our family pork farm in Missouri, we were surrounded by corn—and not just literally. We told corny jokes that left people groaning. People wore clothes we thought were corny—definitely *not* on the pages of fashion magazines. The narratives of many folks sounded corny—tiresome and overly sentimental. But the stories that have continued to resonate with me throughout the years are those my father shared in the everyday moments of farm life. When he shared these stories, he always reminded me that he wasn't an educated man, as he hadn't gone to college. It was years before I truly realized the importance of my father's lessons and fully recognized that he was a much smarter man than almost anyone I knew. Truthfully, I learned far more from my dad's life lessons than I did from academia.

Although we lived in a small, rural area where many people didn't have lofty aspirations, our parents passed along to my four brothers and me many skills and the motivation to use them. My twin brothers are pastors, the youngest brother is a lawyer and law partner, and my other brother is the head of our family farm and the owner of a second business. I met my goal of becoming a CEO by the age of forty. We all had different aspirations, and most of us went our own way, yet we realized it was our solid foundation that gave us the opportunity to achieve our dreams.

I thank my father for that, along with my mother, Marcile, who worked extremely hard to raise us. My greatest hope is that those life lessons I took from the farm, which were a big part of my success and business and that I share in this book, will be passed along to my four children. If that happens, and I believe it will, I will have received far more from life than I bargained for.

Stories continue to be a significant part of my life today. As the president and CEO of Caron, I've had the opportunity to know thousands of addicts in recovery—each with his or her own unique journey. In fact, it continues to amaze me that in the three decades I've been a leader in the addiction treatment field, one of the most powerful messages of these stories is that if they can do it, you can, too.

That message, as I had the opportunity to learn firsthand, is not only applicable to recovery from substance abuse and addiction but to your career as well. I could never have imagined as a young boy growing up on a pig farm that someday I would become a CEO by the time I was forty.

At that time, it was expected that a young person would follow in the footsteps of his father. Since my father was a farmer, it was assumed I would also be a farmer. Perhaps I might join the military or find a career with a church, but the CEO of a major not-for-profit organization? Hardly.

I reached that career goal by applying the lessons I share with you in this book, paired with hard work and dedication. As you read in the Foreword, I entered my own personal recovery after twenty-five years of working in the addictions field. My experience opened the door to an even greater understanding of all those stories I had heard, and a greater appreciation that I could, indeed, achieve balance and sobriety in my life, just as so many others have.

Ultimately, the lessons that apply to life, career achievement, and recovery aren't all that different from one another. The message remains that if I can do it and you follow the same plan, you can do it, too—whether it is achieving career goals, personal recovery, or both.

Like any how-to book, the tools contained within are helpful only if you use them. I believe these tools, when learned and employed, are helpful to individuals of any level of an organization. Whether you're a line person hoping to be a supervisor, a supervisor hoping to be a manager, or a vice president hoping to be president, these tools can help you achieve your goals.

Regardless of whether your organization is not-for-profit, for-profit, large, or small, I particularly hope two groups of people will benefit from this book. Members of the first group are those who work in the not-for-profit world. Many individuals who work in not-for-profits are motivated by an intense passion to help people, but they overlook the role that quality management can offer their organizations.

Business guru Tom Peters once said, "Most quality programs fail for one of two reasons: systems without passion, or passion without systems." Too many not-for-profits have passion but don't have the right types of systems in place, and they fail.

In writing this book, I am also reaching out to individuals in recovery. One of the problematic life issues many of us face is an inability to conceptualize and take methodical steps toward actualizing career goals. If more people in recovery could do this, it would bring them to a new level of success that, ultimately, might benefit the entire addictions field.

Regardless of who you are or what your background is, remember this: it's never too late to develop a plan so that now they will call you "boss."

INTRODUCTION: Get More Than You Bargained For

Why should you read this book? Because it's simple, interesting, and informative. Most important, though, you should read it because you'll get far more than you bargained for.

I grew up on a farm. My four brothers and I were fourth-generation pork farm kids, and we knew farm life wasn't easy. It was a struggle to keep a farm operating under normal economic conditions but even more difficult during the Great Depression.

One way my grandparents managed to hang on to the farm through the Depression was by raising chickens and selling eggs. As students of American history know, this was a cruel time for anyone who had debt. If you couldn't repay your debt, the bank could foreclose on your property, whether it was a business, farm, or residence.

But if you sold eggs every day, you received some cash every day. And some of that cash could be turned over to the local bank, generating goodwill and letting the bank know that you were serious about paying off your debt.

Whenever they could get enough money together, my grandparents would buy more hens, enabling them to increase the flock and the number of eggs they could sell. That was important, because it meant they could pay off more of their debt.

The Story of My Father and the Chickens

One of my father's most important lessons came from an experience when he was sent off on his bike one summer day to the train station to collect delivery of a crate full of chickens my grandparents had purchased.

My dad, who was about twelve at the time, rode the four miles into town, waited for the train, and claimed the Tiemans' chickens, which arrived squawking and flopping about in a wire crate. He strapped the cage to the back of his bicycle and started home.

Everything was fine for the first three miles. After that, however, the paved road ended and turned to gravel. If you've ever ridden a bicycle on gravel, you know that it's tricky. It's especially tricky with a big crate of chickens behind you.

My dad made it about halfway down that gravel road to the farm when he hit some loose rocks. The bike went over, the cage came unstrapped, and the chickens scattered.

If you've never experienced trying to round up a bunch of chickens that have been cooped up for hours on end and now are suddenly unpenned and scared out their minds, you might find it hard to imagine what this was like. Suffice it to say, it was mayhem!

My father's initial reaction, of course, was fear and panic, because he was responsible for those chickens that would contribute to his family's livelihood. Once he calmed down a bit, he quickly realized that he needed help to catch the chickens, so he asked some neighbors and their children to assist him.

It took some doing, but about an hour later all the chickens had been rounded up, the cage was strapped back on my dad's bike, and he was on his way home.

His father, who was a fair but stern man of few words, was waiting for him when he arrived. He simply held out his pocket watch, looked at it, and said, "There must have been a problem."

"Dad, I can't tell you a lie. I had an accident and the chickens escaped, but the good news is that all thirteen are safely back in the cage."

My grandfather scratched his head and said, "Well, that's interesting, since you started out with only ten!"

The Lesson of the Story

My father told me this story when I was young and asked me if I understood the lesson it contained. I was never very interested in the lesson, because I was more intrigued about where the three extra chickens had come from.

I wondered which of the neighbors who had helped him was three chickens short, and if the extra chickens were returned. If the chickens were returned, were they the right ones? Had any of the chickens been injured in all the commotion and maybe unable to lay eggs?

It wasn't until I was in my twenties that I finally understood the lesson of my father's story, which was based on the actions he had taken that day. When his initial panic had passed and my father assessed the situation, he did several things: 1) quickly took responsibility for the problem. Realizing that he would not be able to successfully resolve the situation by himself, he 2) asked others for help. With those who were helping him, he 3) worked hard at addressing his dilemma. Ultimately he 4) got more than he bargained for, ending up with more than what he started with.

When I finally had understood the lesson, my father assured me that this simple four-step process was the key to success in all our endeavors. I realized that learning to apply these principles would shape my very simple philosophy, and I would share that philosophy whenever possible.

Over the years I've found again and again that this lesson holds true. It doesn't matter if you're educated or uneducated, wealthy or poor, working in the profession you prefer or not. You can't assign blame to something or someone else for whatever problem you're experiencing.

It's best to take responsibility for wherever you happen to be and whatever your situation is. My father's message was that it didn't matter that I was raised on a farm or that no one from our family had ever been to college. It didn't matter that we had no cultural or social advantages and had limited financial resources. I was not to use those factors as excuses or blame anyone for my situation. I was simply supposed to take responsibility for my life and figure out how to move it forward.

A key part of what you'll learn in this book will be discovering how to ask for help. While that may seem like a simple concept, it's important to consider *whom* you ask, *how* you ask, *what* you ask for, and *why* you ask.

Most people, especially those who have not achieved what they would like to achieve, have either received bad advice from the right people, or good advice from the wrong people. Or they might have been given bad advice from the wrong people. They have not, however, received the right advice from the right people.

My father taught me how to get the right advice from the right people, and that has proven to be a hugely valuable skill. I want to teach you that skill, as it will be one of the greatest gifts this book will offer.

Good Advice and Hard Work Lead You to Success

Here's something advantageous for you to know. You can get the best advice available, but it won't get you where you want to be if you're not willing to do what needs to be done to be successful.

My father asked the neighbors for help but knew that catching the chickens was his job, as well as theirs. He was lucky that his neighbors were willing to work hard to help him catch the chickens, but it was not their job alone. He needed to work hard alongside them to make the exercise a success.

You'll learn how to enlist people to help you and to work with them to get a job done and done well. You need to learn how to work with others to corral the chickens in the corner and get them back into the crate. That requires you to cultivate a specific set of behaviors, which you also will read about in this book.

Once you learn these lessons—to take responsibility, seek advice, ask for help, and work hard and smart to get a job done—you will find that you have more than you bargained for. Those are the lessons of *Flying Over the Pigpen*. Now let's get started!

*Doug Tieman, age one,
ready to take on the world.*

Mom, Dad, and their four boys in 1964. My youngest brother, Lee, wasn't born yet.

Tieman farm, 2010

*Our family just after I got my high school diploma, 1973.
From left to right, Larry, Lee, Dad, me, Mom, Greg, and Terry.*

Part 1
WANT TO BE

Little League was a big deal in rural Missouri during the 1960s. All the boys played, since there were usually just enough to field a team. Though everybody made the team, not everybody could be a pitcher.

When the coach asked who wanted to pitch, seven out of ten kids raised their hands. I was one of the three kids who didn't. I didn't want to be a pitcher, didn't volunteer to be a pitcher, and, as a result, I never pitched an inning during a baseball career that extended into college.

Sometimes I think back on those years of playing baseball. I think about my four younger brothers, all of whom were terrific pitchers because they had a strong desire to pitch. I wonder what would have happened had I wanted to pitch.

The Lesson

When I teach a class or lead a seminar about leadership, I always begin by asking participants to identify important characteristics they observe in the leaders they admire. I ask them to think of a political leader, someone from the military, a football coach, someone from their company, an entrepreneur, or anyone else who has achieved a high level of success. Then I ask them to list the characteristics that set that person apart as a leader.

Typical responses include the following:

+ intelligent
+ diligent
+ hardworking
+ risk-taker
+ good communicator
+ strong work ethic
+ fair
+ good judgment
+ creative
+ insightful
+ honest
+ integrity

The list could go on and on, but the participant always omits the key characteristic that propels a person to become a leader. The biggest reason someone becomes a leader is because he or she very badly *wants* to be a leader.

The "Peter Principle," a theory of promoting an individual to his level of incompetence, is forty years old but still relevant in some organizations. At Caron, we're deliberate about who gets promoted and why, and we always make sure the person being promoted possesses the skills and ability to handle the job, because we recognize that people who are destined to become true leaders are promoted because they have a strong desire to lead—they must *want* to be leaders. Without that desire, you can't be a truly effective leader.

So the first step to being a leader is *wanting* to lead. If you possess that characteristic, let's get started and lay out a plan for how you can make that happen.

Chapter 1

The Chicken or the Egg?

As my father and I drove through the countryside, we always examined the crops. We talked about the condition of the crops, if they were ahead or behind schedule, and how we thought the yield would be that year. We also made comparisons about whose crops looked better and why.

I was always curious about why one farmer's corn would be much taller than his neighbor's when the fields were side by side. I figured the soil would be about the same, and it probably didn't rain more on one field than the other, so the corn should be the same height.

My father, however, explained the many variables to raising a good crop. You need to consider not just soil and water but the weather, fertilizer, the type of seed used, how the soil was prepared, and when the seed was planted. A farmer can have all the right ingredients for a good crop, but if he doesn't prepare the soil correctly and plant at the right time, he could experience crop failure.

And, as anyone who knows anything about farming understands all too well, you can strictly adhere to all the rules and *still* lose a crop to a variable outside your control. Hail, tornado, disease, insects, and other factors out of your control have ruined many a crop.

The trick, my dad told me, is to understand how to effectively control as many of the variables as you can. You can't stop a hailstorm, but you can control how and when you plant, fertilize, water, and care for your crop.

THE LESSON

Which came first, the chicken or the egg? You learn quickly on a farm that it doesn't matter. As long as you have *either* a chicken *or* an egg and you take the right actions, you'll get good results. It's all about understanding what you have and utilizing it to your best advantage.

The desire to lead is like the farmer's desire to control the ingredients needed for a successful crop. Without the desire, all those other beneficial characteristics and ingredients don't really matter. (An overview of twenty desirable leadership characteristics is listed in Appendix B.)

As with the question of the chicken and the egg, we can ask if leaders are born with the characteristics that enable them to lead, or whether they develop those characteristics. Just like with the chicken and the egg, I argue that it doesn't really matter. Regardless if you're born with characteristics of a leader or you develop them over time, you can still be a leader. You just need to recognize the skills and characteristics you possess and enact the right steps to make them work for you. We all have some characteristics that can be developed into leadership skills. Some of us need to ask for more help and work harder than others, but by *wanting* to be a leader and developing those skills, you can be successful.

Define Your Characteristics

Review the list of desirable leadership characteristics in Appendix B, or make your own list. Now, take a long, hard look at those characteristics and identify—with brutal honesty—which of them describe you. If you sense you don't yet possess the ability to be brutally honest with yourself, I will tell you from personal experience that this skill is a worthy goal. There is simply no value in attributing characteristics to yourself that you haven't yet developed, because that can put you in a position you're not prepared to handle and thereby set you up for failure. It's far better to be honest with yourself and admit you're working to achieve those characteristics.

Once you've identified your leadership traits, think about some other adjectives to add to your list. You may possess qualities and have experienced circumstances that aren't necessary for leadership but will become part of your persona and style, and help define who you are and what makes you unique.

My list of such characteristics and circumstances includes:

+ farm boy
+ one-room grade school
+ of German descent (my one grandfather came over after
  World War I)
+ five boys and no girls in my family
+ musically tone deaf
+ athletic
+ religious and educated in church schools

It's important to identify those characteristics for which you want
to be known. What makes you unique and will help to identify who
you are and what your leadership style will be? As you've no doubt
already noticed, I share my farming background whenever appropriate to define who I am.

That experience tells people who I am and helps identify me as
genuine. Regardless that I've worked with and rubbed elbows with
people in some of the most socially upscale and sophisticated areas
of the country, in some aspects I remain a farm boy from Missouri.
I have never tried to be something I wasn't, and I've learned that
people appreciate and respect that authenticity.

In Summary

The key message of this chapter is that it doesn't matter what
attributes you are born with or which you develop. It does matter,
however, that you 1) learn to identify the characteristics you possess;

2) determine the characteristics you would like to possess; and 3) work toward developing those personal characteristics that make you unique.

You ultimately want to be authentic so that individuals who work for you, with you, or for whom you work will describe you with these same adjectives as you use yourself. When that happens, you will have begun to lay the foundation for your success. Just like the farmer who uses the attributes of his land to yield the best crop, you will not only know whether you have the chicken or the egg but, more important, you'll know what to do with it and you'll strive to do the right thing with it.

Part 2

PLAN TO BE

A s President Dwight D. Eisenhower once said, "In preparing for battle I have always found that plans are useless, but planning is indispensable."

My dad served in the military in the early 1950s, near the end of the Korean War. It was an important learning experience for him, and he loved to share his and other soldiers' stories with me and my brothers. I remember one in particular about a group of soldiers captured by the Russians during World War II who were thrown into a stockade to ride out the rest of the war. The story had become legend and was still circulating when my father was in service.

The story goes that after some time in captivity, several soldiers suggested they develop an escape plan. They had all spent time in the area of the stockade and were familiar with the surrounding territory. They figured that they'd draw up a map from their memories of the area and use it to plan their escape route.

They worked for hours and hours, mapping out the forests, roads, railroad tracks, streams, rivers, fields, and all of the other landmarks they collectively recalled. When they completed the map, the soldiers used it to plan their route, hopefully, out of the stockade and on to safety. Working together they planned and replanned, and eventually they were able to make their escape and arrive safely at their planned destination. Their successful escape, however, is not where this story ends.

A number of years after the war, the soldiers decided to return to the area of the stockade and verify the integrity of the map they had crafted. One of the men had saved the map, and they all were eager to see how closely it reflected the actual area.

To their great surprise, the map they'd drawn from memory was in no way accurate. In fact, it didn't at all reflect the area of the stockade because the soldiers had been told that the location of their imprisonment was different from where it actually was! And yet, they had used the map to secure their way to safety.

THE LESSON

I suggested to my father that the message here must be either divine providence or really good luck, but he disagreed. The moral of the story, he said, is that the plan based on the inaccurate map didn't matter nearly as much as the planning. That this group of soldiers planned together and worked toward a common goal is what made the enterprise successful—not the plan itself.

Even if they'd had an accurate map of the area where they were imprisoned, it wouldn't have benefitted them if they hadn't worked together on a plan. Their common goal and collective effort made them successful. A perfect plan may not be necessary, but good planning absolutely is.

The plan you come up with for your career may not be perfect, either, but developing and consistently working the plan is everything. At Caron we give addicts the tools and the plan to recover from addiction and achieve sobriety and overall wellness. In spite of the tools and the plan, some may experience a relapse. When that happens, the tools and the plan need to be refined. Recovery is indeed possible when mindfully working that plan. Likewise, a successful career is possible for those who utilize the tools and work their plans.

This book provides you with the tools you need to develop a quality career plan that will put you on the path to meet those goals. However, when things don't go exactly as you had hoped, just like those seeking a successful recovery who relapse, you need to commit to refining the tools in your plan. Just like recovery, it is possible for those who remain diligent to have a successful career.

Chapter 2

No Target Is Too Hard to Hit

I was ten years old when I received a BB gun for Christmas. In the 1960s, a BB gun was the ultimate gift for a farm kid because we had endless room to shoot. I was so excited to go outside and start practicing.

My dad took me outside the next morning and gave me a few lessons about the use and maintenance of the gun, most of which I didn't listen to because I was too excited about pulling the trigger. When he had finished talking, he set up several bales of hay, had me stand about fifteen feet away, and told me to shoot at the hay. So I shot and hit the hay bale.

That was easy enough. After a few rounds I was bored and told my dad I needed a smaller target. He suggested we go to the barn, because there were always a lot of sparrows there.

It's not that we enjoyed shooting birds, but too many sparrows were bad for the farm because they brought in disease, ate feed, and generally made a mess.

We found a group of about ten sparrows, and my dad told me to go ahead and shoot at them. I missed, of course, and the birds flew away. When he asked me if I knew why I could hit the hay but not a sparrow, I responded that the hay was bigger, it didn't move, and I'd been closer to it. However, my father disagreed.

He reminded me that when I shot at the hay, I was aiming at *one* target. Yes, it was a big target and easy to hit, but it was just one target. When I prepared to shoot at the sparrows, I aimed at the group and missed them all as they flew away. The point my dad made was that you don't shoot at *birds*; you shoot at *one bird*. You aim for a specific target.

Then my dad took me back to the hay-bale target. I stood about ten feet back and shot, hitting the hay. Then I went about 100 feet from the hay and shot again, missing the target because from that distance it was too difficult. The way to master hitting the hay target from 100 feet, he told me, was to start at ten feet and shoot until you could hit the target nearly every time. After that, move back to twenty feet and master hitting the target from there. In ten-foot increments it would take a while to be able to hit the target from 100 feet, but you'd achieve a lot of goals along the way and eventually hit your ultimate goal.

THE LESSON

I kept this important life lesson in mind as I began to chart my career goals during my mid-twenties. I needed to identify my 100-foot target and then begin mastering it, ten feet at a time. The fundamental message was clear—no target is too hard to hit if you approach it properly and are willing to work hard at reaching it.

It is important to have a goal, whether it is to be a supervisor, manager, director, vice president, president . . . or whatever success means to you. You have to identify a particular target to shoot for or you'll end up just shooting at birds. And it's essential that once you've mastered a target, you set another one and get to work on mastering it (more about that in Chapter 24, Good Ain't Good Enough Anymore).

A very important exercise—maybe the most important—is determining the target for which you will aim. Will it be one you can easily reach, or a far-off one that will require years of effort to reach? If it's distant, what are your intermediate goals? What targets will you hit before you reach your ultimate goal?

Very few people take time to do the personal inventory that is necessary when choosing the target or targets for which they will aim. They don't come to a clear understanding of their goals, so they can't be sure that they're getting where they want to be.

I know lots of people who look back on their careers and feel a sense of accomplishment about what they've achieved. What they don't know, however, is what they might have accomplished if they'd been deliberate about selecting targets and working toward hitting

them. Far too many people make career choices based on convenience, familiarity, immediate financial gain, or loyalty toward an
employer. While these may be factors, they should not be deciding
factors.

Since selecting a target is critical, I strongly recommend you
undertake two exercises. I found them to be extremely helpful to
me in selecting my career path, and I continue to utilize them as I
chart my progress toward new and different targets.

Career Aptitude Test

Take a variety of psychological and interest-oriented tests. They
will provide a clear analysis of your strengths and weaknesses, the
types of jobs you are best suited for, and those you're not suited for.
(See Appendix C for a list of suggested tests.) They are invaluable in
helping you to know and understand yourself.

Armed with a bachelor's degree in education from a religious college, it was only natural that in my twenties I taught high school for
three years at a church-affiliated school. It was an assigned position
for which I didn't have to interview. I was simply appointed to teach
there. I was happy enough with the job because I had assumed for
many years that I would be a teacher and maybe eventually become
a pastor. The problem was that I didn't know in what other employment settings I could excel or what other opportunities might be
available.

After teaching for three years, I wanted to pursue an advanced
degree on a full-time basis, so I applied and was accepted to a PhD

program at a Midwestern university. I left my teaching job in the spring and had the summer off before starting the doctoral program, so I started applying for jobs, hoping to find a way to make some money before heading back to school.

A number of companies I interviewed with tested my interests and aptitudes, using the kinds of tests listed in Appendix C. Much to my surprise, I discovered some incredible opportunities in careers I had never considered. Based on those tests, I selected a sales job for a major floor distributor and discovered that I not only enjoyed it but also excelled at it.

While I learned I was good at sales, I also still had a strong commitment to service work. That meant I would need to find employment that combined these work-related targets of utilizing strong sales skills and serving people.

With both of those targets in view, I possessed more clarity about the type of work I would seek. I was soon able to put my newfound sales ability to use by serving in the fund-raising department of a church-related college. The college used extensive testing as part of the interview process, and once again I learned a great deal about myself and the career options I might be best suited for in the future. I also realized how important it was to craft a strong career plan so I would no longer just stumble into different opportunities. Rather, I would take charge of my career in order to land the kinds of jobs for which I exhibited talent.

Understanding the things you enjoy and the areas you excel in, as well as areas in which you don't excel and don't enjoy, is invaluable in charting a career and making job choices. This knowledge has been critical to my success, as I've enjoyed every job I've ever worked. Being enthusiastic about the work I do generates passion. In contrast to some of my friends who simply work for a living, I can't wait to arrive at work every day. I am extremely fortunate that this quote by Confucius applies to my work at Caron: "Choose a job you love, and you will never have to work a day in your life."

Learn to identify and recognize your gifts, and think about what inspires and excites you. Then set a goal of finding a job you can not only excel in, but is also personally rewarding.

An acquaintance named Ann returned to work in her late forties after having taken time off to raise her children. As a result of her talent, work ethic, and drive, she rose quickly to top positions in the organizations for which she worked. I found it troublesome, however, that she never worked for an organization for more than two years before moving on whenever she found a job that paid more. She would take another job to increase her annual income by about $5,000.

She had a terrific reputation in her field, and many organizations were willing to hire her, but she also had a reputation as someone who didn't stick around. Curious about this, I asked her why it didn't seem important to her to stay with one organization and move up the ladder there. Wasn't she concerned about the collegiality and developing a sense of family that comes from being with an organization for a number of years? I asked her if she was concerned about the reputation she was building as someone who constantly moved along because of income.

Ann told me that she was concerned about the reputation she'd developed, and, indeed, she did appreciate collegiality and familiarity, but there was another side to her story. It turned out that her husband had been a successful executive and they lived extremely comfortably. Ann described herself as a former stay-at-home mother who relished her time taking care of her family and volunteering for work she found fulfilling and valuable. Her husband, however, developed mental health problems, and their financial comfort quickly became compromised. Ultimately, she made the difficult decision to divorce him and planned to return to work.

Ann was then diagnosed with breast cancer and went through treatment and recovery. When she finally reentered the workforce, she had to take financial responsibility for putting her two sons through college. So making the best salary she could was her highest priority. The compensation was more important to her than any type of personal satisfaction or gratification that might come from a particular job.

It's not that she particularly enjoyed changing jobs so frequently, but she was driven by the necessity of caring financially for her family. Her priority was to ensure her sons had good college educations and also save for her future needs. Once I understood that, I was no longer puzzled by or critical of her job hopping. In the end, both of her sons became successful professionals. She retained her successful career and also happily remarried.

Prioritize Your Values

The second part of choosing your target relates to career-related values. Everyone needs to recognize what is important to him or her. To help you with that, I encourage you to make a list of job-related values and prioritize them. What will be most important to you when choosing a job and advancing in it? Do you hope to be able to travel? Will your salary be the driving factor? Will you seek a job that lets you work with animals, or spend time outdoors, or work with disadvantaged families?

Let's look at some of these career-related values. Think about how each one resonates with you, and determine which you feel are more important than others. We do this exercise often with different groups within Caron, and I always encourage staff members to look at the list, think carefully about it, and then rank the values from most important to least important. Feel free to add other values if you wish.

1. **Financial.** This may be the easiest value to describe, as it's something most of us relate to. Financial reward, however, relates to more than your salary. Obviously, you'll want to consider benefits—particularly as health care is such an important factor in the current environment of our country. Consider whether there's some sort of retirement plan, if the employer matches your 401k contributions, if bonuses are included, and so forth. All of these areas contribute to total compensation.

2. **Comfort.** If you're not great at handling stressful situations or don't like change, you probably would do better in a job that provides a level of stability. You might look for a job in which the expectations won't change and the status quo remains the same, work hours that fit your lifestyle, and so forth. If this value is important to you, stay away from jobs that require you to meet quotas or travel often, have high turnover, or demand that you always work under pressure.

3. **Power.** Some individuals feel a need to be in control, make all the decisions, call all the shots, motivate people, and frequently exert influence. If you're reading this book, you likely possess some degree of this value because you're interested in becoming a more effective boss. Other workers, however, shy away from powerful positions because they lack the confidence and assuredness that are necessary to lead. Some people don't prioritize power in the workplace because they would prefer to keep that space simpler so that they can concentrate on family or other nonwork-related priorities. It's important to determine where this value falls on your list.

4. **Convenience.** Some people enjoy having a job that's close to home and doesn't require a long commute, giving them more time to spend with family. Perhaps they could perform some of their work remotely, providing even further work-life balance (though this may depend upon the expectation and structure of an organization). These workers don't want to be required to travel, and they would appreciate a job that comes with a built-in social life with other employees around the

same age and with similar life circumstances. You can define convenience however you want. Understand, though, as with some of the other qualities we're considering, convenience may contrast with other values. For instance, you may have a job that offers all the conveniences you want but comes with a lower salary.

5. **Family.** Working in a high-level, high-stress job can make it hard to balance work and family. Long-distance travel, the need to be available and in constant contact with customers or coworkers, necessary activities outside of work, and other obligations can wreak havoc on your family life. When my kids were young (they are now adults), this family value was extremely important to me. Although my job involved travel as well as evening and weekend events away from home, I always made time to coach baseball, attend school events, participate in family vacations, and just be there for my four children. They knew that they came first and my job second. I engaged them in my job by talking to them about my career, and they were proud of the work I did. My wife and I also made a point to find time to spend together—just the two of us. Take time to think about where this value falls on your list, and remember, as someone once told me, "Your job, unlike your family, will never love you back."

6. **Inner Calling.** Some individuals have a need to serve a "higher cause" and find work that helps others. This type of calling leads people to work for churches or not-for-profits, in health care, education, and other endeavors. This inner

calling was my top-ranked value as I began thinking about my career and the reason I chose to teach in a church-related school. In the early years of my career, I worried that my highest-ranked value of following my inner calling to serve was at odds with some of the other values that were also important to me. These included entrepreneurship, challenge, power, and financial compensation. As I gained more work experience and a better understanding of who I was and what I wanted, however, I realized that those values can mesh very nicely with one another. In fact, the service component can complement some of the other values mentioned. All I needed to do was to keep all of my values in mind as I sought career positions. Choosing to work for a not-for-profit didn't mean I would not have a chance to employ my skills as an entrepreneur, or that I would be financially compromised. I realized I could accommodate all my important values by making thoughtful and effective choices about the types of careers and jobs I would take.

7. **Prestige.** Our society places higher levels of prestige and visibility on some jobs and careers than on others. A September 2014 Harris Poll found that Americans consider the same jobs to be prestigious today as they did when it first started polling in 1977.[1] The order has shifted a bit, but jobs considered the most prestigious are doctor, military officer, firefighter, scientist, nurse, engineer, police officer, clergy member, architect,

---

1 *http://www.harrisinteractive.com/NewsRoom/HarrisPolls/tabid/447/mid/1508/articleId/1490/ctl/ReadCustom%20Default/Default.aspx*

athlete, and teacher. If you enjoy having others look up to you or being considered an expert, this value might be one to consider. Working for a highly recognized and regarded organization also provides a level of prestige. I have gained prestige by working for Caron—one of the most respected organizations in the addiction treatment field.

8. **Entrepreneurship.** Some people are always looking for a better approach. These folks develop new products, improve upon existing products, and change the way we live. While many entrepreneurs start their own companies—an admirable but difficult task—others work within business and industry. Entrepreneurial people are found in every type of career and often enjoy a high level of success. They often possess the ability to take charge and solve hard problems, clear vision, determination, and above-average intelligence. Being entrepreneurial is a terrific leadership attribute, so if this value is important to you, by all means explore jobs and careers in which you can embrace it. Just be warned that most entrepreneurs at some point face criticism, perhaps ridicule, financial hardship, and even failure. The good ones get back up and keep trying until they succeed.

9. **Challenge.** People seek challenge in their jobs for the same reason they climb mountains or run marathons. They crave the exhilaration of overcoming a challenge. They thrive in tough situations and love to prove they can take actions when others doubt them and their efforts. If being challenged is an important value for you, you won't shy away from difficult

job opportunities and you'll be prepared to deal with stressful situations. You like situations in which you have the ability to turn things around and accomplish a lot with a little. You enjoy being challenged and coming out on top.

10. **Interesting/Fun.** I once met a sophisticated, middle-aged man who worked at Disney World. When I asked him why, he said, "Because it's fun." Many jobs, because of their nature, are interesting, constantly changing, never dull, and in some cases just flat-out fun. It's an advantage to be able to make any type of work you do fun, but some jobs are fun by their very natures. I've known musicians, actors, gifted tennis instructors, and others whose jobs are what they most love to do. How great is that? If this value is at the top of your list, you may need to be prepared to make some sacrifices, as some "fun" jobs and careers may not pay that well or could take a toll on family or comfort level.

These are the ten job-related values I have considered throughout my career. Feel free to add other values or take some of these off the list. Regardless of how many values you're considering, prioritize them from most important to least. Then assign each a percentage value, with all the numbers adding up to 100 percent. This exercise will provide you with a good idea of the type of job you'll want to seek, and a good comparison of the relative importance of each of your values.

Making that tough decision between a job that pays more but has less prestige will be easier when you know what you truly value.

Ideally, you should complete this exercise when you are relaxed and not actively seeking a job. If you complete it before beginning a job hunt, you can base your search on those values that are most important to you. Prioritizing your values is a difficult task, and I hope you will not take it lightly.

I also recommend that you complete the exercise several times to see how consistent your list is. Try doing it once every ninety days for a year to see whether the order of your values changes. And you should examine and prioritize your values from time to time as you move along your career path. It's typical that you'll discover the values that were important to you at twenty-five might present as a different priority when you are forty-five.

As you work through this book and begin or continue to develop your career plan, understanding this insight about yourself will make finding the target you want to hit a lot more specific. Remember, when you've firmly established exactly what and where your target is, you'll be far more likely to strike it.

Chapter 3

Being a Copycat Is . . . Good!

As far as I'm concerned, copycats get a bad rap. When I was a kid and wanted to do something my parents didn't approve of, I'd make the argument, "Everyone else is doing it."

They always had the same reply. "Well, if everyone else jumped off a bridge, would you?"

Then there was that copycat joke: "If five copycats were sitting on a fence and one jumped off, how many would be left?"

The lesson was that being a copycat is not a good thing.

How many of us, however, have tried to hold or swing a bat like a certain major leaguer, shoot like a particular NBA star, or replicate the clothing or hairstyle of a certain actor? Maybe the issue shouldn't be about copying but about *from whom* you're copying and *for what purpose.* The goal is to look around at other successful people and then emulate the traits you most respect about them.

THE LESSON

As an impressionable teenager, I was always intrigued by coaches who were hired to coach a team with a terrible record and who, within a couple of years, completely turned the team around. Clearly, the right coach could take the same team of players who once performed dismally and make them into champions. At the time, I wondered what those coaches possessed that enabled them to achieve that type of success. Was it their philosophy or leadership style? Were they just lucky, or was their predecessor a bad coach? What was it? What attributes of those coaches enabled them to be so successful?

Similarly, I was interested in individuals who would take the helm of a struggling company and turn it around. I'd see television documentaries about such business leaders and want to learn more about them and the characteristics that made them so successful. As I closely observed, I was surprised to learn that while most of these leaders shared some characteristics—ambition, inspiration, and competence—others varied widely.

I listed the characteristics these leaders possessed. It turned out to be very similar to the ones listed in Appendix B. Then I considered which of those traits are consistent with my skills and values. I determined to develop a specific style for which I would be known. To do that, I observed other successful people and matched the qualities that enabled them to achieve with my own characteristics. In other words, I became a copycat. You'll find a worksheet in Appendix E to guide you as you compile your list and decide what characteristics will describe you.

I encourage you to study individuals who have been successful coaches, executives, political leaders, volunteers, or other positions. What about them compels others to follow them, encourages people to trust them, motivates people to vote for them, and respond to their direction? When you have an opportunity to listen to a leader speak, don't just listen to the message, recognize the characteristics that enabled him or her to achieve success.

Begin picking out characteristics—both good and bad—of leaders and others you see on the news, encounter in a book or a movie, meet in person, or even follow on Twitter. After a while, you can determine which of those characteristics you already possess and which ones you may want to develop.

Finding the right mentor can empower you to improve your strengths and address your weaknesses. (In the next chapter, I discuss more about the importance of a mentor.) Being a good copycat of those who have done well can be an effective exercise. Determine what style you want to develop and then be consistent and persistent in developing it. Be known by your style, which is based on the characteristics you possess.

Some components of the style I decided to develop for myself include the following:

+ People would know that I grew up on a farm in an unsophisticated setting.
+ Simple values and solutions would be my *modus operandi*.
+ Fellow employees would know me for my honesty, integrity, and work ethic—values I attribute to the farm.

✦ People would clearly see that, like a family farmer, I was willing to get my hands dirty, and I wouldn't ask anybody to do something I wouldn't do myself.

✦ Employees would know me as someone who values the contributions of every employee regardless of his or her position.

✦ People would know me as an eternal optimist and enthusiastic; someone who cares a great deal about employees and would rather tell them the truth, even bad news, than to keep it from them.

✦ Subordinates, peers, and supervisors would know me as passionate, dedicated, compassionate, and loyal.

Over the years, I developed my personal style by watching others, studying the characteristics of leaders, and adopting those that were consistent with my character and personality. I have remained consistent with those, so when others describe me, they cite the same attributes I use to describe myself. While you're developing your style, choose some good role models, be a good copycat, and always be consistent with the characteristics you choose to adopt.

Chapter 4

You Can't Count Your Cows if You Don't Know Where They Are

When I was young, one of my favorite early evening activities was counting cows with my father. We had an eighty-acre pasture. Although the land had some trees, a pond, and a couple of streams running through it, the property was mostly pastureland. Our livelihood came from raising hogs, but we also kept a herd of about 100 cattle. The sight of the cattle grazing on the hill as the sun set in the background was idyllic. I also valued the livestock because it was an opportunity to learn a different skill on the farm. Counting them was an enjoyable task.

On this one particular evening, however, I was a little anxious about counting heads of cattle. I had a baseball game that night and didn't have a lot of time. Running late always made me nervous, which had a negative effect on how I played. I suggested to my dad that this could be a problem, as we'd have to first find the cattle and then account for all of them. And, heaven forbid, what if a few were missing and we had to go look for each one?

My father realized we were short on time, so rather than leisurely looking over all of the property like we usually did, we headed directly to where he was confident we'd find the cows. "How do you know where they will be? We have a lot of land. The cows could be behind trees, behind the terrace, or in the ditches along the streams."

"I know where they'll be today because of the heat and the wind. With the hot weather and the wind coming from the west, the cattle would find a place to stay cool."

"Gee, the cattle must be on the western side of the trees so they could get the breeze," I said.

"Good guess, son, but that's exactly wrong. They'll be on the eastern side of the trees, because when the warm wind blows through the trees, the leaves of the trees actually cool it, creating a gentle, cool breeze on the other side. It works a lot like air conditioning."

Sure enough, we drove to the eastern side of the trees, and there were the cattle. Being a warm day, the animals weren't inclined to run away, so we quickly counted them and headed off to my baseball game.

It's amazing how quickly you can find something when you know where to look. But in addition to knowing *where* to look, it's important to understand *why* you are looking in that particular location. In this case, the variables of wind and heat would have prompted me to look in exactly the wrong place. With the additional understanding of nature my father possessed, however, he was able to go to exactly the right place.

In this chapter, we'll explore how to know where to look to develop the right career—and what to do with what you find.

THE LESSON

In my story, it's clear that had my father not known where to find the cows, we could have wasted precious time looking for them. I suggest that very talented leaders are all around you, and you can learn a great deal from them. I believe strongly that it is important for people who strive to be successful to select a mentor. I was fortunate to select several mentors who helped, and continue to help, guide me along the way.

First, what is a mentor? A mentor is an individual who meets with you a number of times over the course of a year and helps you develop your five-year plan, critiques your progress along that path, and advises you as you make those important and sometimes tough career choices. As I mentioned in the previous chapter, mentors can also help you to better understand and leverage your strengths and develop a plan to tackle your weaknesses. Finding a good mentor can enhance your career.

How do you go about finding a mentor? First, let me advise you about who should *not* serve as your mentor. Do not seek out a relative, neighbor, friend, or fellow employee. You certainly can talk to these people about your career and career opportunities, but they make terrible mentors because they have a vested interest in the choices you make. Your neighbor may or may not want you to move away (depending on the type of neighbor you are). A friend might advise you to work at the same company where she works, even though it's not a good fit for you. All of these people have some type of emotional or personal interest in the choices you make, which does not make them objective or as tough and honest as you need them to be as you develop and work your plan.

Now that we've eliminated the individuals you know best, how do you find a mentor from the remaining 7 billion people in the world you don't know? It's a lot like finding a spouse. You wouldn't walk up to someone you knew only casually, or not at all, and ask her if she would like to be your spouse. You would first develop a good idea of the type of person you would like to be with, then figure out a way to get to know her, and then nurture the relationship—or not. Most of us don't marry the first person we date.

This process allows you to determine your comfort and relationship levels with different people. It allows you to determine the specific characteristics of a person with whom you want to spend the rest of your life. Finally, upon making that determination, you hopefully asked the right person.

Selecting a mentor is much the same, with the good news that, unlike spouses, you can have several mentors at the same time. And if you choose incorrectly, separating is much easier.

The First Step

The first step is to identify the type of person you would like to have as a mentor. The individual should fulfill the following qualifications:

+ be successful
+ have confidence in his or her ability
+ be able to readily talk about his or her management approach
+ have a strong plan in place for his or her career in order to be able to help you with your plan
+ be objective
+ be familiar with the career in which you're interested

The Second Step

Once you're clear on the qualities your mentor should possess, begin looking around your industry or community and develop a list of potential candidates. You can simultaneously connect with people online and then take it a step further and meet with people at appropriate events or one-on-one. You may follow someone on Twitter and determine you really like his approach to work and life. If you see a connection through LinkedIn, for example, who is a personal contact of someone you know well, she might be a possible candidate. But in addition to sending an invite through the social platform, you may want to ask your mutual connection to introduce you.

It's critical to figure out how you can spend time with your potential mentor to get to know him or her and vice versa. If you start with a phone call, e-mail, or a social message, that's okay. Your initial purpose is to start getting acquainted with your potential mentor. I've found that most successful individuals are flattered when someone who aspires to be successful reaches out to them. They are usually happy to share their experiences and expertise.

Once you've become acquainted with a few potential mentors and have narrowed down your choices, ask to either meet in person for the first time (if you haven't already done so) or plan another meeting—again, not unlike dating. If you're looking for a repeat get-together, you could say something like, "Something you said really intrigued me. After thinking more about it, I'd really like to get together again to talk more about it."

After you feel comfortable and have thought the matter through, if you feel she's the right person, you certainly could ask her to become your mentor. Let her know the meetings you've had have been invaluable to you and you'd be appreciative if she'd be willing to meet with you several times a year to talk about your career and where you're headed. Most people are flattered when asked to help groom someone who is serious about advancing in his career.

The Next Step

Once you've lined up one or more mentors, continue to assess the relationships. A mentoring relationship can reach an end for various reasons, or you may feel that you want to find an additional mentor. It's sometimes effective to choose someone within your industry and someone from outside, just for the sake of comparing and contrasting advice and input. So keep your eyes open for a mentor who might be even more beneficial to you as your career progresses because it's possible to outgrow a mentor. (Appendix F provides a worksheet for helping you select a mentor.)

Working with Your Mentor

Once you've established a relationship with the person who will be mentoring you, get down to business about your five-year plan. This will be your road map as you advance in your career, and it's really important that it's sound.

Components of your five-year plan should include the following:

+ A listing of your strengths and weaknesses, based on testing and assessments
+ The prioritized list of your career-related values you'll employ when making job decisions (as discussed in Chapter 2)
+ An assessment of your current career employment situation, including salary, title, responsibility, opportunity for growth, etc.

+ Your vision for where you'll be in five years, including title, financial accumulation, power/authority, and so forth.

Now for the tough part—identifying the steps you will need to take and the best time frames to achieve your goals. Some points to consider are listed below.

+ Will advancement require additional education or train-ing? If so, what would that look like and how long would it take? How will you pay for the extra training or education? Can you be sure it will be worth the investment of time and money?

+ Will you need to leave your current employer to reach your five-year goals, or do you have opportunities to advance within the organization?

+ What kinds of annual advances will you need to make (financial, position, and so forth) to get where you want to be in five years? What are the annual goals you must achieve to reach the five-year goal? For example, if you're currently making $25,000 and in five years you want to be making $60,000, you have identified financial gain as one of your highest job values. However, if the annual raise at your com-pany is 5 percent, you will not reach $60,000 in five years without making significant changes. That means you'll need to identify the type of jobs in which you can earn $60,000, as well as the experience, education, and skills you need for those jobs. If you're qualified, how will you go about locating these kinds of jobs and being a successful applicant?

✦ Developing a five-year plan forces you to assess where you are and what you must do to achieve your goals, while keeping in line with the values you've identified for yourself.

✦ If advancing from $25,000 to $60,000 in five years is your number-one goal, and financial accumulation is your highest ranked value, but your second value is service, you will exclude several jobs because they are not consistent with both of those values. If your family value is third on your list and you determine that you'll need to complete many night-school courses to get the education to move forward to the dramatically higher income, that could also be a compromise.

✦ When weighing all these factors, you might realize that the goal you've laid out for five years from now is unrealistic, sort of like trying to go from a target that's ten feet away to one that's 100 feet away. It might not be possible.

✦ These are the sorts of factors you'll want to review carefully with your mentor and get her feedback on whether or not your goals are possible. If you agree that they are, your mentor will help you stay on track for meeting milestones that will help you to achieve them. She can help you assess your current situation and keep you on track by helping you to develop wise goals and make effective choices toward meeting them.

Setting one-year goals that ultimately will advance you to your five-year goals is similar to the strategy of a long-distance runner. To reach his racing time goal, he sets goals for splits at the quarter, halfway, and three-quarter points of the course.

If he's behind at one of those points, he needs to step up his
pace. If he doesn't, he'll continue to fall behind and not achieve
his goal.

✦ When reviewing your progress toward your five-year goal, it
becomes imperative to keep advancing the goal and working on your next steps. Your five-year goal might change,
depending on how well you're doing in a particular year.
You should always be working five years out. So when you've
completed year two of your five-year plan, you actually will
have planned the next two years and be at year seven. Your
five-year plan is always looking five years ahead of where you
are right now.

I was twenty-seven when I wrote my first five-year plan. As the
plan progressed and stretched out, my long-range goal was to
be CEO of a major not-for-profit organization by the age of forty.
Every career choice I made between the ages of twenty-seven
and forty was based on reaching my goal of being a president
by age forty. I turned down many job opportunities that paid
more or had other benefits, because they didn't move me closer
toward my ultimate goal.

Keeping Your Plan Updated

Updating your career plan is critical. You need to adjust it accord-
ingly whenever you hit—or don't hit—a milestone. If you consistently can hit your target from forty feet but always miss it from fifty,
you'll need to accept that you're a great shooter from forty feet and

not so great from fifty. Unless you prefer a great deal of failure, adjust your plan until you're able to hit the target from fifty feet.

Your plan should always challenge you but not set you up for failure or make it impossible for you to meet your goals. Once you've selected a good mentor(s), rely on her to help you assess whether your goals are realistic and valuable. Not achieving your goals can be discouraging, so make them realistic but also exhilarating. You can't count your cattle if you don't know where to look and how to look for them. A mentor and a five-year plan are essential to a successful career.

Appendix G provides a worksheet for developing, working, and updating your five-year plan.

Chapter 5

Studying Is Okay, Too

As you've probably concluded by now, my family was pretty religious. Daily prayer was an important part of our family life on the farm, and our faith in God was extremely strong. It was our ritual for my mother to listen to our bedtime prayers.

Every night as I bowed my head and kneeled at the foot of my bed, my mother stood in the doorway and listened. Then she tucked me into bed and gave me a kiss.

One night when I was in third grade, I asked God during my prayer to help me do well on a test the next day. I figured that since he created the universe, helping me score well on a test should be easy. "God," I said, "I need your help to do well on my test tomorrow. I didn't study, but I'm hoping you can still help me earn a high mark."

Well, that didn't sit well with my mother at all. She demanded some answers.

"Doug, God's expectation is that we work very hard with the gifts given to us. We do not expect that he takes care of everything for us."

That was an important lesson for me, especially since I didn't do very well on the test! I still pray every day, always keeping in mind that I have a responsibility to work hard, as well.

THE LESSON

The same lesson applies when working toward developing a successful career. Studying and improving on your God-given skills is an important ingredient in success. Everyone should continue to learn. Take courses online or at a local college or university. Go for that advanced management or doctorate in leadership degree. Take a mini MBA course. Read the latest books on how to be successful. Attend seminars or watch motivational DVDs. If exercise, training, refining techniques, and motivation improves physical skills, the same is true for mental skills. At Caron, we encourage all of our employees to continue education and training, and we provide opportunities for them to do so. We partner with area universities and provide some reimbursement for educational expenses to demonstrate our commitment to having excellent employees.

If your company or organization is like Caron and provides opportunities for training and educational advancement, by all means take advantage of them. And if you're serious about getting ahead in your career, prepare to go the extra mile by reading and taking other steps on your own. A few books that I've found helpful are listed with additional resources in Recommended Reading. I encourage you to develop effective interpersonal communication skills. You could take a Dale Carnegie training course or find a course online to help you to feel comfortable in business and personal settings, and improve how you communicate with others.

Chapter 6

Be Prepared to Succeed

My dad liked to use military stories and anecdotes as lessons. The story of Alexander the Great burning his ships was one of his favorites, and he passed the lesson of it on to his sons.

Alexander the Great is considered one of history's most successful military commanders, was undefeated in battle, and created one of the largest empires of the ancient world. It stretched from Macedonia (in present-day Greece) to India. In 330 BC, he invaded Persia. Upon arrival, he ordered his soldiers to burn the ships that had brought them there. When the soldiers questioned how they would leave Persia, their leader told them that their boats were no longer necessary, because they would return home in the boats of their enemies, who surely would be conquered.

THE LESSON

You've already read about engineering and recording a plan for your career, and the importance of continually tweaking and updating it. While you should work with your mentor as you fine-tune and adjust your plan, you also should share it with others—not everyone, but carefully chosen people who will hold you accountable to follow through on pursuing your goals.

Sharing your career plans is the best incentive I know for accomplishing your goals and moving forward. Letting others know about your plan generates self-confidence, which further spurs you on toward success and also holds you accountable. You now expect to accomplish your goals, as do the people with whom you've shared them.

It takes a bit of courage when you first start doing this, so be deliberate about whom you tell. And remember, to maintain credibility you need to meet both your one-year and long-term goals on time.

We've all heard about athletes or astronauts or dancers or inventors or presidents who told the world from a very early age what they were going to be and do when they grew up. Don't you wonder if their early disclosures might have spurred them on to become what they said they would, and achieve more than they might have if they hadn't divulged their plans?

With specific goals in mind and a sound plan to help you achieve them, you will, indeed, be successful. Preparing to succeed even further by sharing your plan with others will give you the incentive to stay on track and perhaps exceed those goals.

Chapter 7

Big Fish,
Little Pond

I loved to fish in the farm pond when I was a kid. It was an average-size pond, about 150 feet in diameter. It was stocked with bass to make fishing fun. We'd pull in bass that weighed maybe a pound and a half and think it was a big deal, at least compared with the little sunfish we'd catch and throw back. To us, those bass looked like big fish.

My perspective on those bass changed, though, when one summer we took a camping trip and fished at the Lake of the Ozarks. There we caught fish that weighed four or five pounds, and many people were pulling in ones a lot bigger than that. All of a sudden those bass we'd been catching at home seemed tiny.

It was then I began to understand the concept of the "little fish in a big pond versus big fish in a little pond" idea.

Small, restrictive environments usually result in smaller fish. Larger environments with better food supplies and opportunity for growth lead to bigger fish. In the right environment and with the proper nurturing, it's possible for a little fish in a big pond to grow into a big fish in a big pond.

The Lesson

Only you can decide what size pond you wish to inhabit and just how big a fish you hope to become. But the concept certainly is something to think about as you make and follow through on your career plan.

The little versus big fish concept applies to business starts in some ways when you apply to colleges. Do you want to try to make your mark at a small liberal arts school, or attend a large university where you might have fewer opportunities to get noticed?

The question continues when preparing to enter the business world. Would you hope to manage a large number of employees in a large setting, or might it be more gratifying for you to become vice president in an organization of fourteen people? Refer to your career-related values and consider how the size of the organization you'll work for relates to those values.

Working as a big fish in a small pond may provide prestige, comfort, and power within the organization. On the other hand, working in a large, competitive environment may offer better financial remuneration, entrepreneurial opportunity, and challenge.

Every company is different in size, mission, and culture. It's important to do your homework and find out everything you can when applying to different organizations. Have a good idea of how you might fit into the company, and determine whether that fit lines up with your values.

Don't be afraid to try working in both large and small settings. Maybe you'll start out in a small organization and find that you're very comfortable there but the environment and work isn't all that exciting. It would benefit you to move to a larger company and see how you fit in there. You could find it exhilarating and challenging to work for a large enterprise, or you may find that you miss the comfort of a smaller organization. Gaining these life experiences early on will give you valuable insights as you plan your career.

Chapter 8

Have an Exit Visa

By and large, pigs are relatively docile animals. They don't attack or seek to inflict harm, especially on humans. However, like all animals, a sow (mother pig) will go to great lengths to protect her piglets. A sow typically doesn't mind if you enter her pen, but if a piglet squeals for some reason, look out. That mom will protect her baby.

A sow can weigh anywhere from 300 to 400 pounds, which is four or five times more than the kid whose job it is to take care of her! Given these factors, from the time we first started helping with the pigs, my father taught my brothers and me that we needed to be *very* careful when we shared a pen with a sow and her piglets. Specifically, he taught us to make sure never to get between the sow and a wall, and to always have an escape route—a plan to get to the fence quickly and get out of the pen. After all, you never knew when a piglet would squeal and how that sow would react.

To be comfortable in the pen with the sow, you needed to know that you were not penned in.

THE LESSON

The worst job in the world is one you feel forced to do. A job where you feel trapped can be a terrible experience. That's why you need to have an exit strategy and the means to leave that job—or at least know that you *can* leave it.

It's only when you're free to leave a position that you're able to stay and be effective in the job. The key concept here is choice. You always want to have the ability to choose to stay instead of feeling forced to stay.

Unfortunately, most workers don't have an exit visa. They feel trapped because of loyalty to the company or boss. Or they think it would be difficult to relocate to another job because their family is tied to the community. Or they feel trapped because they're being paid extremely well and doubt whether they could make that much money anywhere else. The economy also impacts the ability to secure other equivalent opportunities.

People have lots of reasons to stay in jobs they don't like. They get vested in a pension and are reluctant to give up that security, or they can't imagine having to undergo the interview process again. It might just be that they feel needed in their workplace and don't want to let other employees down.

Working in a job where you feel hemmed in isn't good for any-body—not the employee or the employer. If you find yourself in this situation, you need a plan to get out of it. An employee who has a five-year plan is less likely to feel trapped in a position because the plan provides a road map for moving forward. You might feel stuck in one place as you work to achieve something, such as further education and the training necessary to move to the next level. However, understand that you're working to come out on the other side of the tunnel. You're being proactive about finding a better job.

I also believe it's important to complete interviews now and then just to keep your skills honed. Earlier in my career, I applied to and interviewed for different jobs every three years. A bit later, I transitioned to every five years. During the years I wasn't interviewing, I learned everything I could from the company with which I was employed, building up my reputation and skills. Keep honing your interviewing skills to prepare to interview for increasingly complex and competitive positions. You wouldn't interview for a job as a vice president in the same manner you'd interview for a CEO position.

Because I was determined to be in a CEO position by the time I turned forty, I started applying and interviewing for CEO jobs when I was thirty-seven. I wanted to practice those interviews and feel confident that I could be successful. It was all part of my five-year plan.

However, I do not think it's a smart plan to respond to every job possibility that arises. I know people who can't say no to an interview, even when it's for a job they don't think they want. Frequently interrupting your work to interview for other positions requires a lot of time and energy, and can be extremely distracting and counterproductive. Planning on when you'll interview and when you won't can free you from distractions and put you in the driver's seat. You're more likely to excel in your job when you make it—not interviewing for other jobs—your priority.

I worked for another organization for twelve years before becoming CEO at Caron. During those years, I was very clear with my supervisor and human resources about what I expected to achieve, and that I would look for and interview for other positions every three years. Once I had completed those interviews, however, I recommitted to the organization and gave it my undivided attention for the next three years, until it was time for me to complete more interviews. I found it interesting that management was very supportive of my plans. And they always created greater challenges for me within the organization in an effort to retain my services. It's not always possible, but if you can develop this type of relationship with your organization, it can be a beneficial experience. This type of employer-employee relationship doesn't happen overnight. You need to be seen as an important asset within the organization. A word of caution: to have a bold and transparent conversation with your employer requires you to have thoughtfully developed a relationship in which you are highly valued and respected first.

I value every staff member at Caron and would hate to see members of our team leave us to work elsewhere, but I wouldn't try to convince an employee to stay if he or she was ready to move on.

Chapter 9

Interview the Interviewer

There's a legendary story in my home community about a farm family with thirteen kids. The parents loaded all the kids into their truck one day to drive to the state fair in Sedalia, because they wanted to see a world-famous Angus bull on display with the rest of the prize livestock.

When they arrived at the fair, they learned there was a $1 fee per person to view the bull. The farmer wasn't about to pay $15 for himself, his wife, and kids to look at the bull, and he told the proprietor. The proprietor looked at this big family and asked the farmer if all the kids belonged to him. The farmer told him they certainly did.

The proprietor winked and chuckled. "I'm going to let you all in for free. Maybe our bull will learn something from you."

Once the tables had been reversed—figuratively—the family entered the pen and enjoyed seeing the world-famous bull.

THE LESSON

If, like many people, you're uncomfortable with interviewing, you have to learn how to turn the tables, like the farmer did in the story above. By understanding the interviewing process and being prepared and proactive, you'll relieve yourself of a lot of anxiety and be far more successful. Numerous resources exist for improving your interviewing skills, and I encourage you to research what's available. Also, consider taking a sales training course because, when you're interviewing, you're selling yourself. Being comfortable with the process can be very helpful.

Let's look at some of the most common mistakes people make during job interviews.

1. Not researching the organization, the industry, or the position before the interview. These days, it's easy enough to go online and review an organization's website.
2. Lacking questions for the interviewer. (More about this in a bit.)
3. Not anticipating the interviewer's questions, such as how to explain gaps in résumés, job hopping, a backward career move, and other factors. Having well-thought-out answers to these kinds of questions is important.
4. Rambling on too long when responding to questions.

5. Improperly assessing the interview situation. It's imperative to take note of the office environment and the style of the interviewer. For instance, is the interviewer casual? Intense? In a hurry? Does the office environment feel formal or relaxed?

6. Asking about the salary too early in the interviewing process. You should have an idea of what the job pays, because it doesn't make sense to interview for a $50,000 position when you're looking for a minimum of $75,000. You shouldn't ask about the salary until you've been offered the job.

7. Showing up without materials to take notes. It's imperative to take notes.

8. Leaving without a clear understanding of the next step of the interview process, and what you need to do to stay engaged in it.

I've interviewed hundreds of people, and it never ceases to amaze me that, even at senior levels, individuals make many of the mistakes identified above. Not making any of those mistakes will put you light years ahead of most of your competition.

It's important to understand that an interview is not a one-way street. Yes, you'll need to answer a variety of questions, but you'll also need to make several inquiries about the job. Asking questions gives you a degree of control in the interviewing process. You effectively turn the tables on your interviewer, making him or her a salesperson trying to convince you to come to the organization.

It's a bit of an art form to learn when and how to introduce your questions during the course of the interview, because you don't want to alienate the interviewer or appear to be confrontational. As you become more experienced with interviewing, it will be easier to find opportunities to turn the tables and ask the questions you've prepared and have written down in front of you.

The list of questions below are suggestions and not intended to be an exhaustive list. Certainly, you wouldn't expect to ask every one of these questions during one interview. Depending on the position and organization, it's good to have about ten questions prepared for your interviewer. This gives you a level of control and further invests you in the interview process.

1. How long have you worked here?
2. What do you like most about the organization?
3. Why did you come here?
4. What excites you most about the future of this organization?
5. What issues might impede the success of this organization?
6. Who is your competition, and what sets this organization apart from the competition?
7. Can you quickly summarize the company's strategic plan or provide an executive summary I can take with me to learn more about the direction of the organization?
8. Can you tell me about your management philosophy?
9. What would others who report to you say about your management style?
10. What would your colleagues say about you?
11. Can you tell me about how upper management interacts with employees and what style they recommend within the organization?

12. What future opportunities might be available within the company, and what would I need to do to move forward?

13. Why did the last person leave the company?

14. Are any current employees interested in the position for which I'm interviewing? If so, how would they respond if an outsider is hired?

15. How much authority would I have to make personnel changes if some of the staff doesn't fit?

16. What is the budget for this position?

17. How involved would I be in developing the budget in the future?

18. What tools does your organization have for supporting this job?

19. What type of training program does the organization have for my position and my department?

20. What is the culture like in the organization?

When I reached the end of an interview, this next question was the one I always liked to ask. "Based on what you know about me and this position, why do you think I should aspire to the job?"

If you ask this correctly, you'll get your interviewer to convince you that you should want the job, hopefully creating the perception that the company is interested in hiring you. This is a subtle and powerful interviewing technique that requires some practice, making it vitally important that you stay in the game by interviewing for jobs at least every three years. It's the only way you can practice this skill.

The ability to be successful in interviews will be vitally important throughout your career. Take some time to think about how you can avoid the common mistakes listed earlier and how you can stay in control by interviewing the interviewer. It takes practice and confidence but can dramatically increase your chances of being hired.

Part 3
ACT LIKE IT

One Saturday morning, around 10 AM, a man dressed in a suit drove into our driveway. We had completed our morning chores and were in the kitchen eating a snack. When the man knocked on the door, my father went to speak with him.

It was very rare for someone in our area to be dressed in a suit on a Saturday. We made the assumption that he clearly was from "out of town." My brothers and I were quite curious about him and who he was, so we listened closely to his conversation with my father, which went something like this:

"Are the cattle in the pasture next to the road yours?" the man inquired. My dad nodded that they were.

"They are fine looking cattle," the man said, and my father thanked him for the compliment.

The man asked, "How much is an individual cow worth?"

My father said, "It depends."

The man asked, "What does it depend on?"

My father responded, "If you happen to hit one, it would be worth this amount," and he held his hand above his head indicating a high sum. "On the other hand," he said, "if you are the county tax collector, it would be worth this amount," and he held his hand very low.

The Lesson

After the man left, my father returned to the kitchen table and shared the lesson with us. He explained that so much in life depends on one's perspective and that the value of a cow depends on many variables. However, the true value is based on the perspective of the buyer, in other words, what he is willing to pay for it. My father said that life was like that as well; value is derived from the perspective of those observing.

The goal of Part 3 is to help you continue your development as a leader. You likely have not yet achieved all of the necessary skills to be a bona fide leader, but you can act like it. If your peers and subordinates, as well as those above you in your organization, perceive you as a leader, that perception—in other words, your value—can become a reality.

Chapter 10

Promise the Moon and Deliver

When I was a child, we had neighbors who routinely tried to put seven gallons of water into a five-gallon bucket. In other words, they tried to do more than was reasonably possible. While their plans sounded impressive, they always overpromised and underdelivered.

Their sons were my peers, and I enjoyed spending time with them. However, when I occasionally helped them out on their farm, I experienced firsthand the source of their trouble. There is an art to bailing hay, and timing is a critical factor. They would take on a hay-baling job that was too large and, therefore, were unable to complete the work in timely fashion. As a result, they would have to work at night when the hay was tough and damp with humidity. The hay weighed too much, and the hay baler would break down, or the wire or string holding the bale would break. Everyone would be frustrated and the work often wasn't finished. I quickly learned that promising the moon and not delivering disappointed those we were working for, upset us, and did little to inspire confidence. It was clear that continuing on this path would eventually lead to nobody hiring us.

My dad always told me and my brothers to set aggressive goals when we were working for someone but never to promise more than we could accomplish. If we promised 1,000 bales of hay in an afternoon, we should finish the job and ask if anything else needed to be done. If we were to cut weeds out of a twenty-acre field of beans by next Friday, we should try to finish the work by the end of the day on Thursday.

Our neighbors and others we worked for appreciated knowing that when the Tieman boys promised the moon, they would deliver. We became very much in demand as workers because we always delivered what we promised.

THE LESSON

My understanding of the importance of promising the moon and then delivering it goes right back to my father's guidance when I was a boy.

As leaders in business, we need to have that same ability. I've heard people say that the key to success is to underpromise and overdeliver. While that approach is comfortable, easier, and less stressful, it's not going to "wow" anyone. It's simply the safe way. Instead, we need to be able to motivate and inspire, and we do that by overpromising and overachieving.

However, a danger exists in overpromising. Don't do it if you can't achieve it. Anyone who consistently overpromises will not be taken seriously in business. Be sure you know what you're capable of achieving, and try to make sure it's more than what other people might expect. If you are successful using this strategy, you'll be sure to be noticed and earn respect.

When I take on development initiatives for Caron, I often propose goals that are beyond anyone's expectations. If it is the general consensus that we could raise $10 million, I'll propose $12 million. I only do that, however, because I have enough confidence in myself and in my team to be able to promise and deliver. I would never propose that we raise $12 million if I didn't absolutely believe we could achieve it.

The message of this chapter is to look at the proposed goals and figure out how you can exceed them. Don't take the easy route by understating a goal. Instead, exhibit leadership qualities by establishing aggressive, doable goals. If overpromising isn't within your comfort level (refer back to your list of business-related values), you may need to downplay this strategy. Always promise the most you are confident you can achieve. Your peers and superiors will respect your ability to promise to the best of your ability and always deliver. I've employed this strategy throughout my career with significant results. And now that you're a boss, I highly suggest you do the same.

Chapter 11

Be a Mule Skinner/ Cheerleader

When I was a kid we watched the local basketball team play. We were in a small town and usually didn't win many games, but it was still fun to attend and watch. A sense of tradition and history was in that arena, as my father had been a very good player. I knew it meant a lot to him to watch the games with my brothers and me and reminisce about his glory days. As a father, I appreciate that all the more, because I love to share stories about my past with my kids.

One aspect of those basketball games that resonated with me was the cheerleaders. They were always energetic, upbeat, and optimistic, even at the very end of a game when time was running out and we were behind by double digits. They knew we couldn't win, but they kept on cheering their hearts out. And then, after the final buzzer, they shed tears, as if they just couldn't believe the team had lost. Their level of devotion, optimism, and support inspired me.

Some years after those basketball games, I landed my first job as a fundraiser at a college founded by Finnish immigrants. The most instrumental member of the board was a man of Finnish descent who'd achieved a name and fortune for himself as an inventor and engineer. He was a tenacious guy, a characteristic he attributed to growing up in the Michigan mountains, where his father was a copper miner.

In fact, he attributed his success in general to lessons he learned growing up in mining country, just as I attribute much of my success to lessons from the farm. The board member told me that when the going got tough—and it was always tough in the mines—the person you wanted next to you was a mule skinner. He described a mule skinner as someone who was tough, unshaven, chewed tobacco, and wore a leather hat and coat. He was always worn and dirty but tough as nails. Nothing bothered him—not even the mules that didn't want to haul the load anymore. Those mules were no match for a tough mule skinner. According to the board member, the key to success was to be tough, tenacious, and steadfast in working toward your goal.

THE LESSON

At first glance, the cheerleaders and the mule skinner have little to nothing in common. When you think about it, however, they share some important characteristics. They're bound by a common thread of optimism against all odds. Those cheerleaders never gave up, cheering to the bitter end. And that mule skinner wouldn't take no for an answer. Those are characteristics I encourage managers and supervisors to adopt and incorporate into their personal styles.

It's important for people to view their leaders as enthusiastic, energetic, optimistic, and who believe you will be successful against all odds—like a cheerleader. It's equally important that when finances are tight, things have not gone as planned, and the overall situation looks bleak, your employees see you as a leader who is tough and tenacious, with the confidence and skill set to withstand the difficult times and see them through—like a mule skinner.

As a manager, you need individuals to be excited about a goal; that's the time to be a cheerleader and get your team on board. When your organization is facing difficulties, whether financial, an uncertain future, or something else, be the mule skinner—that tough, solid rock upon which your employees can rely. Develop your style and choose when to utilize these personas. You can't be one or the other all the time. A constant cheerleader will not be taken seriously, while a tough, hard mule skinner may seem unapproachable and unpleasant.

Mastering an effective balance of these skills will increase your ability to be a successful leader and garner a reputation for being fair and forthright. Your team will know that you root for them in good times and have their backs during the tough times.

Chapter 12

C-A-R-E

Every farm in the area where I grew up had at least one dog. We cared about our animals, but they were expected to be more than just pets. Dogs on some farms helped herd livestock, others tended to sheep, and those that weren't herders were relied upon to keep an eye on the property.

My favorite farm dog was the very first one I remember: Rex. He had been my dad's dog before my parents were married, so he was our family's first pet. He was a good dog and very useful on the farm. He was helpful with the livestock, but his number-one focus was being a watchdog—and at this task he was extraordinary.

A neighbor ran out of gas once near our farm and walked over to borrow some fuel. Noting that no one was home, he went to help himself from the gas tank that was a fixture of every farm. It was common in our rural, neighborly community for one farmer to borrow from another with the understanding that whatever was borrowed would be replaced or returned. The neighbor had just arrived at the gas tank when Rex noticed him and greeted him aggressively. The neighbor sat on top of the gas tank for a couple of hours until we arrived home to rescue him.

Rex's most notable job as a watchdog, however, occurred during the summer I was six years old. It had rained earlier in the day, and I'd put on my boots and gone outside to jump in the puddles. About an hour later, my mother looked out the kitchen window and realized I was no longer in the yard. She ran outside and saw my tracks in the mud—heading toward the cornfield.

One of the greatest fears of all farmers and their spouses was that a child would get lost in the cornfield. There were miles and miles of corn, significantly taller than a child. Getting lost in a cornfield was cause for panic for both children and parents.

My mother summoned my father and called some of the neighbors to help. People began walking between rows of corn, trying to find me. As darkness approached, my father realized Rex was not around, and he sensed immediately the scenario that was playing out. Rex had seen me going into the cornfield and followed me in. He stayed with me until I eventually became too tired to go any farther and sat down between the rows.

My father ran through the rows, calling for Rex. When Rex heard his voice, he began barking and continued to bark until my dad arrived, only to find me sitting on the ground with Rex watching over me.

The story of Rex underscores the importance of a primary focus. Rex understood that his primary job was to keep the farm and its occupants safe. He would go to any length to make sure he fulfilled his duties.

THE LESSON

What do you care about? What is your priority? In the not-for-profit sector we often struggle with mission versus margin. Our motto at Caron is "Recovery is our only bottom line." We believe it and live it; our very first priority is the well-being of our patients, and our most imperative work is to help them and their families achieve recovery for life.

We understand, however, that we cannot succeed without a healthy bottom line. Every organization, whether for-profit or not-for-profit, must have a solid bottom line in order to produce its product or offer its service effectively into the future. Both are important, because without one, you can't have the other. There must be an appropriate balance between the mission of your work and your expected financial performance. In this chapter, we'll look closely at the mission component of work and how it drives and motivates us.

I believe it's essential to care about what you do. Regardless of whether you work in the for-profit or not-for profit sector, you must care about the people you serve or the product you produce, sell, or distribute. If you teach, you won't be effective if you don't care about your students. If you build a house, you should care about every piece of it. If you run a nationally renowned addiction treatment center center, as I do, you absolutely have to care about every single patient—and every member of their families, as well. If you don't care about your work and what you do, you won't be able to sustain the energy and commitment that's necessary if you want to be truly successful.

In Chapter 2, I noted that my number-one work value is service. With the exception of the one summer I spent selling flooring for a major manufacturer, I have always worked in service industries. During that summer, I was troubled because I couldn't find that service component in the work I was doing. I was good at it, and I sold a lot of flooring. Somehow, though, it seemed disingenuous to me. I didn't really care about the product I was selling. I knew that some of our competitors had flooring that was every bit as good and in some cases better than ours. I could not have sustained the level of sales expected of me because I didn't really care about the job.

I believe everyone should take a long, hard look at the work they're doing and ascertain whether it's something they truly care about. Evaluate your level of passion for what you do. If it's not there, it's doubtful you'll be able to achieve the level of success you hope for. Take a few minutes to once again review your career-related values from Chapter 2 and think about whether your current job really reflects those values.

Not everyone is cut out to work in the service industry or in a caring profession. That doesn't make someone a bad person or a lesser individual; it just means that he or she needs to choose another field.

We all have different skills and interests. Being in the right field is of critical importance if you want to achieve your highest level of success. Having worked nearly my entire career in the not-for-profit sector, I have a passion for caring professions. It just feels right to me to work in that type of setting. But whatever career path you choose, make sure you care about what you do. Have a passion and consider your job to be Job One, just like Rex did.

Chapter 13

Sin Boldly

If you've never had occasion to drive a nail through a piece of tin, you may not be able to fully appreciate this story, but stay with me. There are always a lot of chores to do on a farm, and occasionally one would involve nailing a piece of tin onto a wall or roof or some other place.

The tendency when nailing tin is to hold the nail to the tin and choke up on the hammer, taking small, cautious swings at the nail. The problem with this approach (I can tell you from personal experience) is that there's not enough pressure to put the nail through the tin, only to make the hammer bounce around. This doesn't accomplish the task and often results in a smashed thumb.

Once your thumb has been smashed, the tendency is to employ even more caution with the hammer, which, of course, means that the project most likely will not succeed. However, someone who knows how to nail tin will tell you that the trick is to hold the hammer at the end of the handle and take a full swing at the nail. This forces the nail to easily pierce the tin while avoiding the thumb.

Nailing tin can be compared with several aspects of life. If you acquire some instruction about the task and then proceed with energy and conviction, the results generally will be successful. If you begin a task without direction and work hesitantly, a great deal of pain can be inflicted.

THE LESSON

I sometimes think about Martin Luther's concept of "Sin boldly," which he adopted from St. Augustine. "Sin boldly" is an instruction to be decisive and live with a level of gusto because God is a forgiving God. I like that concept, and I think it's relevant to management.

Having worked in large and small organizations, I've repeatedly witnessed "paralysis by analysis." Days, weeks, sometimes months can pass as decisions are deliberated and debated to death. People are sometimes so afraid of making a bad decision that they make no decision at all. Groupthink can be a valuable tool but not when it highjacks the task or mission at hand.

Over the years I've come to believe that, in most cases, the only bad decision is indecision. Sure, every now and then someone will make a spectacularly bad decision that comes with spectacularly bad consequences. Usually, however, there are no truly right or wrong decisions, just decisions to make and then deal with. Many times we can't know what the right decision is until after the decision has been made.

The Myers-Briggs Personality Test (see Appendix C) revealed that I am very willing to make decisions with few or no facts. That means that I will make a decision I believe to be reasonable and then find facts to support it.

If you haven't already done the personality test, I suggest you do. It will help you understand your decision-making, management, and information-processing style. Understanding your style enables you to put a team in place that balances it. If you, like me, are willing to make quick decisions, for instance, you'll want someone on your team who is very deliberate about decision making.

Decision making can be difficult, but it's a necessary part of being a leader. Leaders need to be decisive. Individuals view decisive people as insightful, intuitive, and bold. That doesn't mean they're always right, but they need to be able to take action. And when they make a mistake—as will happen—they need to assess the situation and figure out how to fix it and move ahead. Don't make excuses or try to blame someone else. Take responsibility for the situation and be prepared to propose an alternative. Everyone makes mistakes. What's important is that you learn from your mistakes. Don't let them paralyze you, just use the lesson you've learned and move on.

In my mind, someone who has never made a mistake has never taken a risk. And risk is necessary for a company to advance and grow. Clearly, taking foolhardy risks is never wise, but being decisive is a trait of a leader. Get to know your decision-making style. If you're reluctant to make decisions, surround yourself with team members who will provide the input you require in decision making.

At Caron, every decision we make and every action we take is patient centered, and we must always be willing to err on the side of the patient. Our patients expect the very best, and we need always to be prepared to deliver. Training my staff to make timely and necessary decisions on behalf of our patients ensures that we'll offer the best care possible. If staff members weren't able to act, patient care could be negatively affected, and that is not an option.

Decision Making and Meetings

Have you ever heard this definition of a meeting? "A meeting is a lot of smart people sitting around in a room trying to be smart with each other." If not, you probably can relate to the definition, anyway. I understand that meetings sometimes are necessary, but they also can be a colossal waste of time. I challenge you to think about this the next time you're in a meeting. If information that is critical to fulfilling the mission of the organization is not being shared, or if the meeting is not for the purpose of decision making, it probably is not useful or necessary. The productivity of an organization increases dramatically when unnecessary meetings are eliminated. Empowering members of your team to make decisions can sharply decrease the need for meetings and dramatically increase productivity.

At Caron, we use a tool when making important decisions. You can see a copy of it, called Action Plan, in Appendix H. We developed this tool because we used to have trouble determining who should be responsible for making various decisions, resulting in no decision being made because no one wanted to offend anyone else.

The decision-charting tool designates roles for various team members as related to decision making. Someone is assigned "the V," which designates that person as the ultimate authority and decision maker with Veto powers. If the decision affects the entire organization, I get this designation, but in many cases it is given to a department head or someone else in authority. A manager, or "M," also is designated and is responsible for implementing and carrying out the decision once it's finalized.

A third person (or people) is given a "D," and designated as being *directly* involved in discussions relating to the decision-making process. Another individual or group is given a "C," for Consultant, and charged with fact-finding and providing input concerning the pending decision. Still another person or group is identified as needing to be kept *informed* regarding the decision, and assigned with an "I."

This might sound complicated, but it streamlines every decision-making project by making clear the roles of every member of the team. Everyone understands their jobs and the question of leadership is clearly defined. We utilize the decision chart at every meeting at Caron, and it is one of our most valuable tools.

When I arrived at Caron in 1995, we undertook a substantial campus redesign. We relocated offices and departments to achieve greater efficiency, causing significant confusion and angst among employees.

The logical move to me was to give the V to our Director of Plant and Operations because he best understood how the campus operated and the moves necessary for making it operate more efficiently and effectively. I also gave him the M and assigned him as project manager.

Everyone impacted by the campus redesign received a D, or *directly involved* designation, providing them with a level of input regarding their needs, where they preferred to be moved, and what sort of space they required. Our architect and CFO were designated as Cs because we needed their consultation regarding design and budget. Those needing to be kept Informed, or the I's, were others within the organization, including some of our vendors and customers who would need to be kept up-to-date about where individuals and departments were located.

This decision-charting tool was a new concept at Caron, so I made sure I communicated to staff members my expectations and how the process would be set into motion. Still, nothing proceeded as I expected.

During the first two weeks of the process, I was consistently lobbied by individuals and departments as to why they needed particular spaces or locations. I would listen carefully, and then ask why they were talking to me, since I was not in charge of making the final decisions. Their answers were always the same. At Caron, they'd tell me, the president always made the decisions.

It took me a couple of weeks to convince my staff that they needed to be lobbying the Director of Plant and Operations, because he possessed the V and was ultimately responsible for decisions concerning the campus redesign. They were initially surprised, and perhaps a bit put off by the decision-charting process, but they saw evidence that it worked, and our redesign was successful.

The decision-charting form helps us to all stay on the same page as far as our roles in decision making, and it charts deadlines, as well. Effective decision making is critical to any group or organization, whether it's a household, a start-up, or a Fortune 500 company. Developing good decision-making techniques among your team and within your organization will move your company ahead and empower you to act with authority.

Chapter 14

Reach Out and Touch Someone— or Everyone

AT&T, then known as the Bell System, had a popular and successful advertising campaign during the 1980s in which it urged customers to "Reach out and touch someone" by calling friends and loved ones on the telephone. The message was circulated by poignant, feel-good commercials depicting people calling others—not to ask for anything or report news—just to express love and concern. Viewers were advised to "Reach out and just say hi" and stay connected.

One commercial depicted two families who had met on a camping trip and happily kept in touch afterward by calling each other. In a different commercial, a daughter in college alarms her parents by calling unexpectedly. The parents are concerned about the reason for the call, because in those days long-distance calling was relatively expensive and many people used it only when absolutely necessary. The parents answered the phone and prepared themselves for the worst when they heard their daughter on the other end of the line (this was long before Caller ID), probably anticipating bad news. It turned out, however, that she had just called to tell them she loved them.

They must have been really good commercials, because I remember them thirty years later. (You can find some of them on YouTube.)

We have many other ways of staying connected today, most of which are positive and useful. I enjoy using Skype to keep up with my kids, and we save a lot of time and money at Caron with video conferences, which eliminate the need for travel. We find social media to be a valuable tool for keeping in touch with our constituents, and our website enables users to chat with a counselor if they have questions about Caron's services. We also employ a My First Year of Recovery program, which is a private, online social platform personalized for former patients and their families. The program includes follow-up calls from Caron staff to patients and family members, online connections, and other services enabling Caron and former patients to stay in touch as well as for Caron to provide support.

Meaningful communication, by whatever means you choose, is not only a profound social tool but a valuable tool for business leaders. Effective leaders are able to communicate in a way that is important and affirming to team members. Just like the college student who connected in a meaningful way with her parents by reaching out to them by telephone, you can make valuable and inspiring connections with members of your team.

THE LESSON

A study by the Harvard Business Review *listed* the top ten motivators for employees seeking high levels of job satisfaction. One might think money made this list, but it was number eleven. The top ten were: achievement, recognition, the work itself, responsibility, advancement, growth, supervision, relationship with supervisor, and work conditions (more about this in Appendix I).

As leaders, we often don't get the most from our employees because we don't motivate them to achieve and recognize their achievements. We don't "reach out and touch" our employees, and thereby we don't inspire them to work toward their full potential.

Employees want to know when they have achieved something. They want to be praised and to feel good about their work. They want responsibility and accomplishment, and all that comes from good oversight by an effective supervisor.

Take another look at the top ten factors that contribute to employee satisfaction. Can you see how they're all linked? And all of them are based on good communication between employees and management.

While e-mail and texting are efficient means of communicating, sometimes you need to get on the phone or walk over to someone's office for a face-to-face talk.

Remember that communication is a two-way process. While it's the job of management to provide instruction and direction to staff, it's also our job to encourage feedback from employees and to listen—really listen—to what team members say.

Taking time to get to know your employees on a personal level also will go a long way in making them feel valued and motivated. Take a minute to comment on a family photo and learn about their family members. Find out what an employee aspires to and where he or she hopes to go within the organization. Don't be pushy or intrusive, but let employees know you care. Caveat: In today's day and age, it's important to be mindful of your organization's social media culture and policies. It may not be appropriate or professional to "friend" your colleagues on Facebook.

Not achieving some level of connectedness makes your job as a leader a lot harder. If you don't have a relationship with your employees, your direction and leadership is not as effective. If you praise someone for a job well done, it seems hollow because there's no relationship behind it. If you reprimand or correct someone for work that is not what it should be, the employee is likely to be responsive because you're missing the connection that's necessary for a meaningful boss-employee relationship.

Supervisors sometimes use their power and authority to intimidate and hold people emotionally hostage for mistakes. It's much better, however, to reach out to a team member in a positive way that helps him or her grow. The level of loyalty from employees who believe you want to help them succeed is immense.

An important consideration is that you can't reach out to *some* employees—you need to reach out to *all* your employees. Every member of your team, regardless of how many, should feel like you have a personal interest in how they do. If your organization is small, you won't have a hard time getting around and checking in with team members. When I arrived at Caron, there were about 200 employees, all at one location. I soon knew everyone's name and was able to greet everyone personally when I encountered them.

Caron now has numerous locations and nearly 1,000 employees, and it's no longer possible for me to know every person's name. I still work hard at making personal connections, however, by taking steps, such as gathering team members in small groups. Anything you can do to demonstrate a level of caring for your staff and show your appreciation for the work they do will pay remarkable dividends.

Following are suggestions for making employees feel appreciated and motivated:

+ Attend new employee orientation and meet new staff members.
+ Send new employees a "welcome aboard" letter signed by you.
+ Attend department meetings to let employees know you're interested in their daily work.
+ Invite groups of employees to CEO lunches.
+ Make your presence known by walking around and talking with people.

✦ Eat lunch in the employee cafeteria, making a point to sit
with different groups of people and chat with them.

✦ Offer all-employee meetings at times that are convenient to
staff members, not just for you. Caron is staffed around the
clock, so I've offered meetings at which we share strategic
planning, year-end results, and so forth as early as 6 AM
and as late as 8 PM to accommodate workers on all shifts.
I believe this shows sensitivity and commitment on my part,
and they respond.

✦ Offer cash awards for innovations that either save or make
money for the organization. Employees are motivated to
come up with creative ideas when they know they'll be
recognized for it.

You can take many other actions to reach out and touch employees. Be innovative and creative, and develop something that is consistent with your style. E-mail blasts and social media can be valuable
tools for staying connected. Regardless of how you choose to make
connections, be consistent and reach out to everyone. And remember
that once made, connections need to be maintained.

Chapter 15

Be a Winning Coach

I always enjoyed helping my father with the evening chores. He was a patient and kind teacher, and it was fun to feed the livestock and keep an eye on what was happening on the farm. As I became older, he allowed me to drive the tractor, which I loved, and I took on increasing levels of responsibility.

Right before the start of fourth grade, my dad sat me down for a talk. He was going to do some combining (for those of you who didn't grow up on a farm that means using a combine to harvest grain) for our neighbors and wouldn't be around at night to do the chores. As a result, I would be responsible for the chores, and my three younger brothers were to help me. I was excited about this, as it would give me the opportunity to be in charge and direct my minions in accomplishing the evening chores.

The first night, I gathered my brothers together and we headed off to do the chores. The oldest of my younger brothers was going into second grade, and the twins would be first graders when school started. To make a long story short, the first night of our chores was truly a disaster. It wasn't that my brothers weren't willing to listen to me; they had been told they were supposed to help me. It's just that they didn't respond well to my barking orders to them about how much grain to feed the cows, what types of protein to give them, which pens to clean first, and where to get the water. It was all very confusing to them, and they were overwhelmed. Work that normally took my father and me between thirty and forty-five minutes took nearly two-hours for my three younger brothers—and I'm not sure we did it right even in that amount of time!

When my father returned later that evening, he asked how the chores had progressed. I told him they hadn't gone well because my brothers didn't do what I asked them to do. I said they didn't understand anything and that, overall, I didn't believe they were that smart or effective help. Then my father asked me if I had showed them what to do and how to do it, as he had always done with me. I hadn't thought of that. He also asked whether I had given them appropriate tasks considering their age and size. I hadn't thought about that, either. Dad suggested that I think about what would be appropriate tasks for each of the three boys. "Maybe, you should show them how to accomplish the tasks in bite-size steps so they would not only understand but could readily replicate that activity. Showing, demonstrating, and helping them be successful would be far more effective than just telling them what to do."

That night my dad gave me my first lesson in coaching.

Another valuable lesson in coaching came to me a couple of years later in gym class. The teacher told us we were going to learn to juggle, which was pretty exciting for kids. However, what we really were going to learn turned out to be far more valuable than juggling skills.

The teacher divided the class into three groups. I was assigned to the first group, and the teacher told us that, surely, we'd seen people juggle, so we should go ahead and figure out how to perform the feat. In other words, we were told to "just juggle." Members of the second group had someone show them how to juggle and help them. Finally, members of the third group had someone who showed them how to juggle and also demonstrated a series of steps to master. When they mastered each of the steps, they could then put those steps together and juggle.

Well, you can imagine the results of that class. No one in the first group could juggle. By watching and listening, several people in the second group were able to juggle a little bit. In the third group, however, everyone could do simple juggling. And they had a grasp of the art of juggling through the series of steps they'd been taught. This had a powerful impact on me. I hadn't learned how to juggle, but

I had learned the importance of not just telling someone to do something but of demonstrating how to do it and, most important, breaking down a task into manageable components that can be replicated. In other words, I learned the lessons of being an effective coach.

THE LESSON

Over the years I've thought about learning to do chores and then teaching my brothers how to do them. I've also thought about that juggling class. I believe the lessons learned between those experiences are as follows:

+ It's important to realize that different people (for instance, my brothers of different ages) possess different levels of abilities, so appropriate assignments must be considered.
+ Telling is not coaching.
+ Telling and demonstrating can be helpful, but for some people—remember group two of the jugglers—it will not be effective coaching.
+ Telling, plus demonstrating, plus dissecting the task into doable components constitutes effective coaching.

Let's take a closer look at those important lessons. First, consider the reality that not all employees are created equal. A wide variety of theories divide the workforce into different levels. I like to consider the workforce in three broad categories, with the understanding that abilities within those categories will vary. Some folks will be at the top of their level, while those who are at the bottom may not be significantly different from the top of the next level. The three broad categories are as follows:

+ The Superstar
+ The Steady Eddy
+ The Marginal Employee

Depending on your industry and the level of your department within the company, between 5 and 20 percent of your staff could be Superstars. Obviously, the more of these employees you have in your ranks, the better. These individuals are the easiest to coach. They're thirsty for more responsibility and are the overachievers. Superstars are excited about establishing goals and proving to themselves that they can accomplish their goals. They bond well when achieving goals and appreciate recognition from their supervisors. They are excited by the work itself as well as being given more responsibility, advancement, and growth. The best way to compliment these individuals is to continue to offer them more responsibility, provide praise, and present them with challenges. Discuss their potential for career development; help them to think about their futures and to find a mentor. Show them that you're interested in their advancement, provide them with constructive feedback on how they can improve, and promote them!

The Steady Eddy typically will make up the bulk of your employees, probably between one-half and two-thirds. I often refer to this group with a baseball analogy, saying that this is the .280 batter who hits fifteen to twenty home runs a year and drives in eighty runs.

They're not all-stars, but you can depend on them year in and year out. Steady Eddies aren't flashy but are steady and reliable and in many ways the backbone of your department, company, or organization. While they're not Superstars, they respond to many of the same incentives as Superstars. Don't confuse them with Superstars, however, because expecting more than they're able to provide is a sure way to frustrate an employee.

Once you determine who this group is within your workforce, it's important to realize that they'll need more coaching—like the individuals in the third group of jugglers. Tasks will need to be broken down into meaningful and understandable components. Continue to work with them, show them how to undertake tasks, and help them be successful. Praise them for successfully accomplishing tasks, and provide coaching tips and feedback on how they are doing. Help them to have realistic expectations of where they can expect to go within the company, and provide challenges so they continue to grow and advance. Be careful not to advance your Steady Eddies too rapidly, as they will balk and become frustrated if they feel they are incapable of fulfilling expectations. Do, however, provide enough challenges, opportunities, training, feedback, and effective coaching to keep them motivated and invested, because these workers are critical for your organization.

The Marginal Employee should make up less than 10 percent of your team—hopefully less than even 5 percent. The reality, however, is that they're there. Some Marginal Employees may have personal problems, or they may have health or other types of issues. Regardless, it's important to realize who they are and how you can be an effective coach to them. The first thing to realize is that you're not a psychologist, psychiatrist, doctor, therapist, counselor, or clergy member. If an employee appears to be suffering from some sort of disorder or experiencing difficulty due to a serious personal problem, they need help. No amount of effective coaching will help these types of issues. Your job as a manager is to note that the employee's performance, attendance, or behavior is not what is expected. With appropriate documentation and assistance from the human resources department, refer this individual to an employee assistance program or another program within human resources. Based on performance, attendance, behavior, or a combination of all of those qualities, you will become aware that an employee is experiencing a problem. As the person's boss, however, it's not your job to fix it.

Then there are those employees who give you other types of problems. Some appear to be lazy, while another might be frustrated about being passed over for a promotion. Some seem never to do the job quite right or finish their work on time, while others are negative toward their coworkers. In these cases, it's important to give employees very clear and appropriate tasks, with clear expectations regarding quality and timing. And it's essential that all of these instructions are well documented. You should have a strategy for moving Marginal Employees into the Steady Eddy category, making them team members who are able to pull their own weight. If you're not able to motivate or convince them to improve, begin working with human resources to develop a plan for their exit. Negativity, habitual tardiness, and not doing their fair share should not be tolerated, because that sends an incredibly negative message to the remaining 90 or 95 percent of employees. When these traits are tolerated, it establishes a low bar for the rest of your team.

Marginal Employees, for whatever reason, are not going to understand how to do something simply by being told to do it. They need to be given bite-size tasks and shown how to accomplish them. When they do, treat them like a Steady Eddy by providing appropriate praise, since all employees appreciate achievement and praise. Develop with them an appropriate plan on how they will continue to improve their skills. If they are incapable of this, make it clear that they may not have a future with your organization, and pursue the required documentation and human-resources department involvement.

With all employees, it's important to develop an appropriate coaching plan for their level. It's essential to determine what they're capable of doing at the very beginning of their employment. Don't just tell someone what to do, but divide the task into understandable components and demonstrate how it is to be done. Provide praise, help team members to achieve their goals, and provide appropriate advancement. Deal with mistakes as opportunities to demonstrate how to do a task correctly.

My young brothers eventually learned how to do their chores correctly because of the simple advice my father gave me. You can use that same advice to become a great coach to your employees. When you're known as a great coach, great players will want to be on your team, making both you and your employees winners.

Chapter 16

Lose the Battle, Win the War

One summer when I was growing up, a drought impacted our entire community. I learned more than one lesson during that dry summer when I helped to move cattle from one area of our property to another so they could have water. Occasionally, a dog or noise would spook the cattle, causing the herd to stampede. Believe me when I tell you that fifty to a hundred cattle charging off in a particular direction is way more than a handful of youngsters with a few sticks could negotiate. My father told us that when this occurred, we should simply let the cattle go. "Don't chase them. Just let them run it off."

Once they had run until they were tired, we would find them, round them up, and bring them back. It was clear that it was far more effective to yield to the stampede and corral the cattle later. Once they were corralled, we could lead them where they needed to be.

LESSON

Too often we let our egos get in the way. We have to be right. We have to win the argument. We have to demonstrate how tough we are. A wonderful skill to learn is how to lose a battle but finish as the ultimate victor. Let me explain.

I learned the value of this strategy while working as a mid-level manager in my previous organization. Many mid-level decision makers reach stalemates over meaningless agendas, even though at the time they seem critically important. People in these positions are so concerned about being right and wanting to do it their way that they can't see the negative end result.

I developed a strategy to deal with this problem. When I was a mid-level manager and it seemed like something could not be effectively resolved, and we were not making headway toward a solution, I would say, "That's fine. We'll do it your way, and I'm in full support of that." By doing this, I was earning chits for something that would be more important to me later on.

Another way of looking at this strategy is that it's choosing your battles. When you are in a situation in which there are differences of opinion on what to do, choose your battles wisely. If the outcome doesn't matter all that much to you, and you think a more important showdown is coming later, don't fight the current battle.

A classic case of knowing when not to fight occurred when I was a mid-level manager at my previous organization. A colleague from the finance office reported that the *Wall Street Journal* would no longer be delivered to our department every day. Instead, the newspapers would stay in the finance office and we'd need to retrieve them. Well, someone who worked for me had a terrible problem with this and suggested that I should use my muscle to ensure the papers continued to be delivered to our department. I had a brief conversation with my counterpart in the finance department and realized that was not going to happen, so I let the matter drop.

My subordinate suggested that I was weak and should have fought more aggressively, even suggesting I should have gone over the finance person's head to continue delivery of the papers. I remember telling her that I had progressed pretty rapidly in our organization by not fighting the unimportant battles but winning the important ones. I told her that while I was sure there would be a time when we would need to use muscle with the finance department, it certainly would not be over the delivery of the *Wall Street Journal*. Save your power for when you really need it.

"Save your power for when you really need it" became a motto I've tried to instill in everyone with whom I have worked. Whenever a disagreement arises between departments, I encourage my coworkers and staff to question whether it really matters who wins. If it doesn't, then don't waste time debating, arguing, or stewing about your differences. Let the person or team who feels the strongest about the matter make the decision and move on. If it really does matter, that's when you'll need to utilize all of your persuasive skills and not back down.

I've worked with many individuals who spent inordinate amounts of energy winning battles but kept on losing the war. It's very important to discern which decisions are critical and make sure you have the tools in place to address them. It's also helpful to train your staff to select battles wisely. Far too much energy is spent debating mundane or relatively meaningless issues and topics.

Look around your department or organization and identify issues that have resulted in unnecessary battles and wasted time. These issues might involve parking spaces, lunch breaks, starting times, office space, and so forth. These are the battles that keep you from focusing on the war—the real reason you are in business. Be a big-picture person and pay attention to what is really important—providing the best products or services possible. Forget the battles, but be sure you win the war.

Chapter 17

Cut Your Losses

The uncertainties of raising a crop made it easy for me to decide early on that I did not want to be a farmer. Every year something affected the crop: too much rain or not enough rain, too hot or not enough sun. Some years destructive insects or some type of disease hit the crop. There could be hail. There were birds. Our livestock might invade the crop. If any of these issues occurred early enough in the growing season, we simply plowed the damaged crop under and planted again. However, if the problem—whatever it was—happened too late in the year, it was questionable as to whether we'd have enough growing days before the frost. When that happened, my father said we would "Cut our losses," and not raise crops on that particular plot of ground.

Or we might not cultivate or spray the crops on that acreage so as not to add additional expenses but simply look for another way to utilize the ground and make it an asset for the farm. For example, if not enough rain was the problem, we might allow the livestock to graze in the affected area. If the crop had no nutritional value, we might let it grow just so it could be plowed under in the fall and serve as a fertilizer for next year's crop. It was important to calculate during a disaster how to compensate for the misfortune and be certain not to invest more to achieve nothing. Farm life, with all of the uncertainties of nature, helps one understand that the skill of cutting the losses just might be one of the most important financial decisions to learn.

THE LESSON

While this seems to be an obvious extension of the Sin Boldly and Lose the Battle, Win the War chapters, I believe it warrants taking time to address the fact that when the situation is not going as planned, it's important to know when to cut your losses. Cutting your losses is also sometimes necessary when you've made a wrong decision, or when you're engaged in a battle you simply can't win.

When cutting your losses, it's all about timing and understanding how to turn defeat into victory. Let's be honest. If you sin boldly and take risks, you will make some bad choices. Like a farmer, you need to know when to plow the field under and plant another crop, when it makes sense to allow your cattle to graze on it, or when you plow it under for fertilizer.

Realize that defeat is certainly not easy, especially for a mule skinner who takes pride in hanging in there when the going gets tough.

But once you've done all you can, tried your hardest, and see that the situation is not going to work out, make a decisive move and cut your losses. It's critical that you're not wimpy about doing so—be decisive and accept full responsibility for the situation. You can justify why you made the original decision while accepting the fact that the situation didn't work out the way you had hoped. Then explain why you are making the new decision and take responsibility for the new direction.

It's hard to know how long to wait before cutting your losses. It's natural to want to wait and see if the situation might resolve itself or turn around. Maybe next week will be better, or next month, or next quarter. I believe that any time you need to make a decision that requires use of resources, it's important to establish benchmarks that must be achieved within a certain period of time. That can make it a lot easier to know when to cut your losses. For example, if an initiative was supposed to generate a million dollars in the first quarter and it generated only $750,000, you certainly have a platform on which to make the decision to cut your losses. What if, however, other people believe the trend during the past month was good, and you're sure to hit your second-quarter benchmark? Then you have a decision to make.

Often, even when they're falling short of the benchmarks, people continue to pursue a goal because they can't admit failure. When you cut your losses, you're admitting that you were wrong, and that's a hard thing to do. Sure, you can be a mule skinner and hang in there and ultimately turn the situation around, but you need to think about the time and energy required to do that, and ask whether it's worth it. Sometimes your energy is better redirected elsewhere.

Regardless of what you decide to do, make sure that everyone knows it's your decision and you're taking responsibility for it. Sometimes you will fall short, and the best thing you can do is readjust and develop a new plan. Cutting your losses doesn't mean you're a loser.

Cutting to the chase, the critical lesson of this chapter is how to cut your losses and look smart while doing so. This again pertains to the type of style you'll develop for yourself. My style in these situations is to get personal, rather than acting like cutting my losses is just another task to take care of in a busy day. When a project of mine didn't work out as planned, I take several actions. First, I demonstrate that I had gathered the appropriate data and solicited good input from key people before ever starting the project. I thank everyone who worked on the project and acknowledged how important it was. And then, after explaining how I had agonized over the decision, I say that it is time to change course regarding the project, because doing so is best for the entire organization. If the decision to cut our losses means individuals need to be displaced or removed from their positions, I inform each person individually, demonstrating genuine remorse and concern. I believe it is a leader's responsibility to make difficult decisions and deliver difficult news.

I hadn't been at Caron too long when I was talking with a new employee. I asked where she had come from.

"I was laid off from a major employer in the community as part of a 250-member reduction action," she said.

"How did that feel to be laid off? How are you coping with it?"

"Though it was a difficult experience, I feel worse for the chairman/CEO of the organization than I do for myself."

It turns out that the chairman had shared how personally painful it was for him to have let these employees down and to see them leave. He hoped that someday the organization would be in an economic position to rehire and perhaps they would want to come back.

"He was visibly moved by having to share that bad news with us. I felt great compassion toward him," she said.

I thought this was a wonderful tribute to a chairman/CEO who had demonstrated his care and compassion for his workforce. Even when he had to deliver tough news, employees respected him for taking the bull by the horns and doing it himself. He could have delegated the unpleasant task, but he did it himself, thereby earning respect and admiration.

Cutting your losses can yield ultimate gains because it enables you to redirect your energy and resources in a positive way. Once you've done so, however, be sure that you're even more diligent and effective, and muster all of the leadership skills you have to make that next effort as successful as it can be. Cutting your losses is sometimes necessary and can be a useful technique, but it should be used as sparingly as possible.

Chapter 18

Be Authentic
All the Time

Church life was very important to my family. Regardless of how busy we were—and certain times of the year, like during planting and harvest season, my dad was extremely busy—we would not only take time to attend church but also to be active in its activities. As a result, my father would often use the church and religious stories as teaching tools. The story that follows about a wealthy farmer who dies and is waiting to be admitted into heaven was one of those stories.

Saint Peter met a wealthy farmer at the pearly gates of heaven. The farmer proceeded to tell Saint Peter about all of the wonderful charitable things his farm corporation had done to help so many people. Saint Peter complimented the man on his corporate acts of charity but wanted to know what the farmer had done personally to help the less fortunate. The man thought and thought and then remembered that once, while in the city, he encountered a vendor selling pencils for three cents. He gave the man a nickel and told him to keep the change. Another time, when an orphan was selling apples for a nickel, he gave him a dime and told him to keep the change.

Saint Peter inquired whether that was all that he'd done personally, and the farmer said that was all he could remember. Saint Peter suggested that he would need to talk with the Almighty about the man's fate. He went off and came back a little while later to relay God's verdict: "Here's your seven cents, now you can go to hell."

The story is a powerful message about *pretending* to be charitable versus actually *being* charitable. The farmer used his corporation to appear charitable, but he had no charity in his heart. He wanted to be perceived in a certain way, but it did not come through with his actions. God saw through him and so did people. Any values or qualities you believe to be important must be for real, or they will, indeed, be transparent.

THE LESSON

This chapter is all about being authentic. Whether you are religious or not, it is essential that you examine your values and determine who you really are. We spent considerable time looking at your work values as they relate to the type of job and career you wish to pursue, but it is equally important to shape your workplace personality and values.

The best leaders possess certain characteristics, as listed in Appendix B. These include integrity, fairness, honesty, forward-looking, and a sense of compassion. Identify the characteristics and values for which you wish to be known, and utilize them in all of your dealings and relationships. Those characteristics can be part of your persona only if they are genuine and you display them all the time. For example, if you want to be known for your integrity, you must do the right thing all the time. That doesn't mean you can't ever make a mistake, but you must always, as much as it's humanly possible, be true and hold fast to doing the right thing.

I have a motto that if something is right, it's right all the time. It's not dependent on the situation. Since honesty—with integrity as an integral ingredient—is the number-one trait of most admired leaders, make my motto your mantra. Don't try to be clever or sneaky or get one over on people; make your word mean something. If you promise to do something, don't rearrange the meaning of that at a later time so that you don't have to follow through on your promise.

Aspire to act with honesty/integrity all the time. Other values, such as second-ranked "forward-looking" and third-ranked "inspirational," can follow. In Chapter 3, you ranked your work values from one to ten in order of importance. Using the form in Appendix E, rate your values and characteristics for which you'd like to be known. Include them in your plan and make them part of what you do every day. When employees and colleagues describe you as having the attributes you include on your list, you'll know that you've achieved an authentic style. You are who you say you are, not a wealthy, callous farmer trying to pass himself off as a charitable giver.

Be perfectly clear about your style and values, and be consistent and persistent. When you live those values all the time—not just when it's convenient or comfortable—they become part of who you are, and you will live an authentic life.

Chapter 19

What About Your Boss?

In addition to helping out on our own farm, my brothers and I often worked for other farmers. Farmers who didn't have kids, or whose kids were grown and had moved away, were always looking for reliable help, and my brothers and I were likely candidates. We were hired to bale hay, walk beans (cut weeds out of soybean fields), or drive the tractor to cultivate, plow, or haul grain.

Some of the farmers were great to work for, while others were less desirable. The ones we enjoyed working for were personable, paid us well, and provided good meals and snacks. Others could be grouchy and, to tell you the truth, a little bit stingy. My father, however, didn't let us pick and choose whom we worked for. If somebody needed help, we were expected to help. He challenged us to see what we could learn from every farmer we helped. If nothing else, Dad said, "You might learn how *not* to do something."

As always, my father knew what he was talking about. I learned a lot from the farmers I enjoyed working with, but I also learned from the ones whose company I did not prefer. I learned how *not* to treat your help, how *not* to perform certain farming chores, and even how *not* to approach life. My dad knew these would be valuable lessons, as we'd be working with and for different types of people throughout our lives. He knew we'd have some great supervisors and some not-so-great ones. It would be nice to pick and choose our bosses, but, as you know, it doesn't always work that way.

THE LESSON

When starting out in a new position, I assess my boss by preparing a grid. Please note that you can follow along with the example of my grid in Appendix J. To complete this exercise, I draw a line down the center of my paper from the top and one intersecting horizontally, forming a cross. On the left side of the paper I write Leadership Qualities. On the top of the grid I write Personality. In the upper left-hand grid I draw two plus signs. On the upper right-hand side I write a plus sign and a minus sign. Likewise, on the lower left grid I write a negative sign and a plus sign, and then in the far right I put two negatives. The assessment of my boss falls into one of these four grids.

The upper left-hand grid is where you want every boss to be, as it indicates that he or she has good leadership skills and is willing to share them with you. It also indicates that this individual is enjoyable to be with and learn from. An upper right-hand corner boss possesses effective leadership skills but, for whatever reasons, doesn't have the type of personality that gels with yours. This type of boss isn't overly interested in coaching you, and your time together won't be as enjoyable as you'd like. However, you could still learn from this individual.

The lower left-hand corner boss has marginal leadership skills but is a person whom you'd enjoy being with. He or she is helpful and interested in seeing you succeed and is at least nice to be around, but has an inflated opinion of his or her abilities. A boss who falls into the lower right-hand corner is obviously the worst situation—someone with limited leadership ability, as well as someone you wouldn't enjoy spending time with. This boss has little interest in coaching or being helpful to you.

Making a boss assessment grid within thirty days of your employment helps you to determine what your boss is like. You will still need to reassess every year, as your initial assessment might have been inaccurate or circumstances could change. Evaluating your supervisor is valuable to you in several ways. If your boss has marginal leadership skills, you want to approach what you are learning carefully. Unfortunately, very few people take the time to learn how to be a leader. You are learning leadership skills through this book, but most people pick up their leadership skills from their supervisors.

Everyone tends to pick up leadership traits from their bosses, whether they're effective or not. Some undesirable traits leaders pass along include the following: dictatorial, autocratic, withholding the truth, manipulative, short-tempered, verbally abusive . . . you can fill in the rest. I've seen all of these traits passed along, particularly during stressful times. One needs to beware of these types of behaviors and make a conscious effort not to adopt them. When the going gets tough and stress levels are high, it's very easy to fall into that trap.

Now that you've assessed your boss, let's look at some strategies for learning all you can.

Grid 1. ++ Positive leadership skills and positive personality type—obviously, this is the ideal. You can talk to this boss about your career and receive open and effective commentary on your strengths and weaknesses, along with a meaningful critique of your plan. Don't confuse this type of boss with your mentor, but similarities will exist in the two relationships. When your boss falls into this category, it is easier to follow through on some of the tasks I have suggested, such as interviewing for jobs every three years and keeping your interview skills fine-tuned. Bosses in this category are not threatened by your initiative. In fact, they encourage your growth. They understand concepts like the exit visa. They know that when you are free to leave, you also are free to stay and likely to become a terrific employee.

Supervisors can become your champions within the organization as it relates to promotions, pay raises, and increased responsibility. They can coach you on the types of actions you should be taking to improve yourself within the organization, such as attending specific classes, volunteering for a special assignment, or attending an important meeting. This individual might even become a friend with whom you'll interact socially. But be careful. As a boss, I'm always wary about developing too close a relationship with any work associate, but that attitude varies from person to person. Make sure to keep appropriate boundaries. While you certainly want to be friendly and do work-type activities together that are social, I would not become friends outside of work or via social media. Make sure your relationship remains professional—albeit friendly and sociable.

As you move on to other areas of responsibility within or outside of your organization, continue to discuss your career with this individual. Should you move outside the organization, this individual could certainly become a mentor once he or she is no longer invested in you as your boss.

Grid 2. +– Positive leadership skills but negative personality type—this type of style is easy to identify. These people are often standoffish, guarded, suspicious, and reserved. They have effective leadership skills, but, because of their interpersonal relationship skills, they are not comfortable spending time with individuals, sharing much information, or developing relationships with anyone on staff.

These types of bosses can be very helpful, particularly if you can approach them from a logical and business perspective. Their assistance will help you do a better job so that you can help them—if that is your desire. I once worked for an individual like this. We made a strategic pact, spelling out what I would do for him and what he would do for me. He had an excellent perspective of his limitations, so it made perfect sense to him that while he taught me leadership skills, he would learn about personal interaction by observing my actions. We were extremely comfortable working together in this manner, and during the three years I worked for him, he taught me more than any other boss. We didn't develop a personal relationship—it was all business—but I am extremely grateful for the leadership lessons he taught me.

Grid 3.–+ Marginal leadership ability coupled with terrific interpersonal communication skills and relationships—this is a somewhat common combination. The problem is that too often people within the organization are attracted to the personality type and overlook the leadership deficiencies. These bosses were promoted because everyone likes them, creating the misperception that they're talented leaders. It's important to recognize that while this type of boss is nice to be around and cares about you and wants the best for you, he or she probably has limited ability to teach you. Be cautious about hitching your wagon to this type of boss, because eventually he or she will be promoted to a level of incompetency and ultimately fail. Being too closely aligned with someone like this can not only be detrimental from that perspective but also because of what you'll learn while working with him or her. Separate the positive, such as the value of developing interpersonal communication skills, from the negative. This type of boss often overestimates his or her competency while wanting to help you succeed. Be cautious about adopting the boss's leadership style, but do take a lesson from his or her interpersonal skills.

Grid 4.--- Negative leadership style and negative personality type—my first question for you is, why did you take the job? While I believe you can learn something from everyone—even if it's how not to supervise—I also know that it takes a great deal of resilience to prosper in a dysfunctional situation. If you find yourself in this situation, make sure you have an exit visa. You must not be trapped in this position. By having an exit visa, you position yourself to possibly turn this negative situation into a positive one by exerting your leadership. Be a shining star within the department.

Regardless of what type of boss you have, effective ways to work with him or her are available. Read the strategies below. They'll help you to make good use of your time and often impress the boss.

✦ **Getting started.** It's good to learn right off the bat about your boss and the expectations he or she has for you. You don't want to be too aggressive, but it won't hurt to ask your boss questions about his or her background, such as academic degrees, training, work experience, tenure with the company, and major accomplishments. You might ask about challenges for the department/company, short- and long-term plans, and so forth. Then ask your boss to tell you about his or her expectations of you. Ask how the boss prefers to communicate. If you have a problem, should you show up in his or her office or use e-mail? How will you know if you're on the right track? How does the boss delegate? Are you encouraged to take risks, even if they may lead to mistakes? I always want to know the ground rules, and I've found that most bosses are happy to share them.

I shared with my bosses the type of feedback, communication, and supervision I needed. If my bosses met my needs in those areas, I would go through a brick wall for him or her. Being clear about both your boss's expectations and yours is advantageous to everyone. Now that I'm the boss, I employ this strategy with direct reports and encourage my staff to do the same with their teams.

+ **Have an agenda.** Always show up to a meeting with an agenda. Depending on your boss, it might not be a bad idea to provide him or her with the agenda ahead of time. A typical boss does not like surprises but likes knowing the purpose of a meeting. Whether it's a routine meeting or a special one called by either you or your boss, make sure you have an agenda. I once had a boss I rarely saw but who routinely called me on the phone. This boss taught me the importance of always having "a boss discussion list" on hand. He was very busy, and when he called, he expected me to be able to rattle off a handful of items we needed to discuss. Having that list at the ready meant we always had an agenda from which to work.

+ **Take notes at meetings.** I always take notes at a meeting, and I don't understand why everyone doesn't. The decision-charting tool discussed in Chapter 13 is an effective means of note taking. Electronic devices also are handy and an easy way of storing notes. However you choose to record them, meeting notes help you to stay on track with what happened and also to follow up on various action items and decisions. Passing your notes along to your boss with comments about how you plan to accomplish action items is sure to impress and minimizes the possibility for misunderstanding.

+ **Limit meeting times.** If you have a meeting with your boss, be efficient and businesslike. Once you've completed your meeting agenda, move on. If your boss is highly interpersonal and wants to socialize, follow his or her cue, but don't let it go on too long. Once your meeting with your boss is over, make it clear that you're heading back to work. At the beginning, you might want to establish a time frame for the meeting. Asking how much time you have when you arrive at the meeting allows you to gauge how long you'll spend discussing various agenda items. Take care of priorities first and be clear on the length of the meeting. When you've covered the agenda, get back to work!

+ **Try to limit interruptions.** You're meeting with your boss about some important matters, and her phone dings with a text message. Distracted, she checks the text and sends a quick one back. This happens two or three more times, and you're starting to feel frustrated. Then her cell phone rings

and she signals you to wait while she takes the call. What
are you to do? It can be uncomfortable sitting there while
someone else talks on the phone, plus it's taking up time during which you could be doing something else. If your boss
takes calls during meetings—and, full disclosure, I am one of
those bosses—initiate a conversation regarding ground rules
for phone calls. If you have important business to discuss,
or a lot to cover in a short amount of time, communicate
that and ask if your boss could forgo taking calls until you've
finished your conversation. Most bosses, me included, would
be okay with that. If your meeting is routine and you have
ample time, let it go.

If your boss takes a phone call that drags on and shows no
signs of ending, you might pass her a note saying you're going
to check your messages or send a couple of e-mails in the hall-
way outside of her office while you're waiting. That usually
will elicit some type of signaled response. Phone etiquette has
changed dramatically over the past decade, and, though it's
great to be connected, being available by phone all the time
can be a real distraction. If phone calls or texts make it impossible to complete meetings, have a conversation with your boss
about the best approach for both of you.

✦ **Make the most of your annual review.** Your annual performance review should be a win-win for you and your boss.
Your boss can talk about positive work you've done, and
you can feel good about what you're hearing. The review,
however, should include ways on how you can improve.

Too many people, both bosses and their direct reports, don't spend enough time preparing for the annual review. Take this event seriously, and, regardless of how annual reviews are conducted within your organization, make sure you've done your homework to chart the results of your efforts from the previous year.

If you use a strategic planning document, have those results with you during your review. If you had specific goals during the year, be ready to share how you achieved them. If you received recommendations for areas in which you needed improvement at your previous review, have documentation prepared on how you worked to make those improvements. Do the same for outside training or education. Be prepared with documented facts of what has occurred since your last review. It's a good idea to take a copy of your current job description and some notes regarding what you've done in each of those areas over the previous year.

An annual review also is an opportune time to discuss whether or not your job description accurately addresses the work you're doing. Many times, employees who are on an upward track tend to do more than their job descriptions call for. Your annual review is the perfect time to call attention to the additional areas of responsibility you've assumed and suggest that it might be time to improve or update your job description. Many people I know don't have an updated job description; they know that they are outdated, but they don't take the initiative to make sure it's up-to-date. At Caron, it's mandatory for employees to update their job descriptions following their annual reviews. It's important because it demonstrates to the employee and the organization that you each value the work being done and take it very seriously.

Discussing your job description with your boss during your annual review is a great way to keep it updated. Stay on top of it and make sure that it happens. Often, bosses are busy and annual reviews are put on the back burner or are rushed through. If your boss does not address your review in a timely fashion, be proactive and ask to schedule a time for your review.

Employee reviews should be conducted more than once a year. At Caron, I do reviews twice a year, but I know other bosses who prefer quarterly reviews. Regardless of how many times you're reviewed during the year, make sure a system is in place for evaluating your progress and performance. This can enhance your relationship with your supervisor.

What If Your Boss
Is a Board of Directors?

If you work in the not-for-profit sector, as I do, your boss might be a board of directors. This is a very different situation from having a single boss. I hope you will read this section even if you don't work for a not-for-profit because you could someday be asked to serve on a board. As you aspire to leadership, you need to be prepared to give back, and serving on a not-for-profit board is one way of doing that.

Developing an understanding of the relationship between a not-for-profit board, the chief executive officer, and the staff will also serve you well for that time when you serve on the board.

Not all boards are created equal. There are many types of boards, with a variety of purposes. For more information about them and the roles they play, consult the Recommended Reading at the end of the book. Also, reputable consultants help not-for-profit boards and their executive staffs to understand and be successful in their relationships. Boards can range in size from a few members to dozens. Members of some boards, called working boards, conduct some of the work for the organization. For instance, an accountant who serves on the board for a small not-for-profit might do the financial work for it. Other boards, called policy boards, have no involvement with day-to-day activities; they simply establish policy for the organization.

Regardless of the type or size of board or how often it meets, you must understand several fundamentals if your boss is a board of directors. This section does not address board size, structure, composition, or frequency of meeting, for those factors vary dramatically by organization type. If you are interested in those topics, read some of the resources given in the Recommended Reading, or utilize the services of a not-for-profit board consultant.

If you work in a not-for-profit organization, one area of analysis and evaluation in your strategic planning process should be your board. However often you do strategic planning, board evaluation should be part of it. You need to learn if the current board structure and makeup is appropriate for where the organization is right now. Too often, boards stagnate and thus no longer suit the organization.

The important basics to remember regarding a board of directors are as follows: The board's role is governance: it sets policy and determines the type of work the organization will do. Board members determine the mission of the organization and develop the strategic plan. They also hire the chief executive officer. The board's role is *not* management—it is not responsible for running the organization. That is the responsibility of the staff. It's critical the CEO ensures that the board and staff fully understand their roles. Responsibilities must be clearly defined and adhered to. If they start to bleed over, trouble can occur. Let's look at a few examples of this.

Suppose an organization is experiencing financial turmoil, and staff presents to the board that a downsizing must take place. The board establishes a downsizing policy, authorizes management to eliminate $100,000 worth of salaries, and approves the appropriate severance and outplacement package for the laid-off individuals. The staff then implements that policy by determining who is to be terminated, what firm will provide the outplacement services, and how that message is to be delivered. The board *cannot* then tell management it disapproves of some of the individuals who will be let go or that it would prefer they use a different outplacement service. Board members may not criticize the manner in which the staff informs employees of the downsizing. It was the responsibility of the board to set the policy for a downsizing of $100,000, but implementing that policy is the responsibility of management and staff.

In another example, suppose an organization is experiencing rapid expansion, and staff brings a proposal to the board to add 20,000 square feet of space, which would include twenty additional beds and appropriate support areas at a cost of $1 million. The board authorizes the construction of such a facility. It establishes policy regarding the building's appearance, size, and structure, but it is the staff's responsibility to develop plans that conform to that policy. Staff members select an architect to develop the appropriate plans for the building within the scope approved by the board. The board will then approve those final plans. If board members don't like them, they make recommendations on what needs to be done for the plans to be approved, and staff goes back to the drawing board and tries again. It is typical for boards to establish a committee structure to provide input, and it is also common for the executive team to seek advice, counsel, and input. Board members may not come back to the staff and tell them how to implement those plans. They can't decide which contractor or architect to use, or which office goes where. Yet boards too often find themselves in the middle of those types of decisions, and it certainly complicates life for the CEO.

Because it's easy for the lines to blur, it's imperative that the chief executive officer and the board annually review who has the V, the veto—just like in decision charting. Whose role is it to make the decision? If it's policy, the board makes the decision. If it is implementation of the plan, it is the responsibility of the staff. I visit with many of my CEO colleagues around the country who work with not-for-profits. Clearly, boards that insert themselves into matters for which they have little or no expertise cause more problems than any other issue. Because boards set policy, they can require staff to take actions that are not in the best interest of the organization. These can include vendor selection, staffing patterns, promotions, physical appearance of the facility, information to be included in brochures, and how the website looks. A strong chief executive of a not-for-profit must clearly outline what the board can and cannot do.

When new members come on to the board at Caron, we have an orientation and clearly outline the role of the board and the role of management. This also is a good opportunity to remind incumbent board members of the basics. Areas of concern to keep in mind include the following:

+ **Staff-based relationships.** Inform board members that although you understand they are friendly with some staff members, and they may visit or talk to staff members in general about the business of the organization, conversations dealing with specifics are out of bounds. If a staff member has an issue, a concern, or a recommendation, he or she should utilize the appropriate chain of command within the organization. Board members address critical issues through the appropriate board channels and not with individual staff members. Both staff and board members must understand and abide by that distinction.

+ **Hiring board members as staff.** Doing so is sure to create conflict and confusion among both board and staff members. Someone who was once your boss (as a board member) is suddenly your subordinate. This may happen from time to time in smaller communities, but I try to avoid it at all costs. If it is necessary, interview the individual only after he or she has resigned from the board. There should never be a situation in which a sitting board member applies for a position within the organization. Should a former board member be hired, his or her new role as an employee must be made very clear, along with the understanding that he or she no longer has a role or relationship with the board.

+ **Bringing on a former employee as a board member.** Similarly, this can also create an awkward situation and should be avoided. A CEO is the boss of the employee. When the person is appointed to the board, however, he or she is now the CEO's boss. A former employee also tends to have strong staff relationships, which can blur the line between governance and management. This individual would serve as a funnel for employee concerns to the board, which then involves them in management issues in which they have no responsibility.

I have many personal preferences about how a board should be composed and the level of diversity and variety of skill sets it should include. These preferences, however, are based on my organization's needs and may be very different from your considerations. Do you need a board that has fund-raising capabilities, or one that's dedicated to your cause? Should there be term limits? Develop a plan for your board. Whether you have a mediocre board you want to develop further, or a terrific board you want to maintain, you should have a strategic plan for how to continually improve it, just as you have a strategic plan on how to progress your organization.

I believe the most important work a board does is to approve a strategic plan. Board involvement in the strategic planning process varies from organization to organization, but it should definitely be involved in approving one. Your strategic plan is the road map for what your organization does. When the board approves that plan, anything within it gives the chief executive the V. You have the right to make decisions within the confines of that plan. Anything outside of it is the responsibility of the board. So if the plan talked about a $20-million budget for a specific project, you have the power to develop a plan within that budget. If you're looking at a $24-million plan, however, you'll need board approval before you can move in that direction.

Your strategic plan becomes the measuring tool against which the executive reports. I have identified critical success factors from Caron's strategic plan. I see these as the important strategies, actions, and appropriate measures that allow us to measure against the plan, and I report them to the board's executive committee at the next scheduled meeting. If we are not meeting some of the goals, I include an explanation for the deficiency. Should something be chronically deficient, the plan needs to be revised. Developing this reporting tool is an effective way to keep board members away from the more mundane operational issues and keeps them out of management.

Involve board members in the development of your organization's strategic plan, developing a tool to effectively communicate the results against the plan, making sure you hit the goal. This will help to keep the lines between the board and management clearly defined and can eliminate a lot of problems.

Conflict between board members and management typically occurs around these two areas: finances and employee morale. If there are financial problems or employees aren't happy, you can be assured that one or more of your well-meaning board members will begin spending more time on campus, and suggestions on how to improve the situation will become mandates. If you cannot rectify that, it is time to look at your exit visa.

If you find yourself in conflict with your board, seek an outside facilitator from a not-for-profit board consultant group to come in and help. However, the first approach should be to try the strategies listed above before conflict becomes an issue.

If you are not in a not-for-profit environment but are serving as a board member, or plan to serve as one in the future, I hope you are very aware of the difference between the roles of the board (governance and policy) and management (decision making). Avoid the temptation to become involved with decisions that are the responsibility of management. If you are displeased with the role or the effectiveness of your CEO, you may need to look at a different chief executive.

As the chief executive, it's critical you provide the agenda and background materials at least a week before board meetings so that the board can review them ahead of time. This is a reasonable expectation, and it is not your responsibility to review or read that information at the board meeting. I also believe it's useful to have various committee chairs and volunteers offer reports, rather than having just staff report. It is appropriate to have the type of committee structure in which board members are aware of proceedings because they've received reports from their particular area of involvement as it relates to the strategic plan, and can give an accounting on the strategic direction of the organization.

Board meetings also give board members the opportunity to share their ideas and input. An effective CEO learns how to balance board members' participation in policy and governance decisions, and to allow a critique or question as it relates to information provided in the board material distributed prior to the meeting. If you have questions about your board meetings, occasionally an outside facilitator's review of how this works can be helpful.

Unfortunately, many board meetings become ineffective and nobody realizes it. The focus of board meetings should be on strategic governance. If the board is becoming involved in making operational decisions, the meeting is heading in the wrong direction. If that's a possibility within your organization, the chairman and CEO should undertake an audit of the entire board-meeting process and board structure. Board meetings need to be interesting and stimulating, and they must ultimately advance the mission of the organization. If not, you'll have a difficult time recruiting and retaining strong members. If nothing changes, valuable board members simply will become uninvolved and stop attending meetings. People who want to make a difference want to be at meetings that also make a difference. Therefore, having effective, productive board meetings is a worthwhile effort.

Finally, as chief executive officer, who is your boss? In some organizations it's the entire board. In others, it's an executive committee, or a compensation committee, or the chairman of the board.

Whoever it is, make sure that everyone is clear on that matter. Establish ground rules on how you will communicate and how you will be evaluated. Remember that board members are volunteers, so it's vital to establish these guidelines and make sure you're evaluated regularly.

Organizations do contracts differently, but I encourage CEOs to ask for a contract that coincides with the strategic plan. If your organization has a three-year plan, you should have a three-year contract that parallels the plan. The contract would cement that as long as you're achieving the goals of the plan, you are there for the duration. There should also be a clearly defined and timely automatic renewal. Again, attorneys can develop ways for either party to exit the contract, but it is important for a CEO to know that he or she is there for a specified period of time and has the stability needed to successfully complete the strategic plan.

As far as negotiating salary, I have found that using a compensation expert to do a review of similar positions has been a helpful way to maintain a competitive salary as well as appropriate benefits. I also believe that part of the CEO salary should be "at risk," which means a bonus plan is in place for achieving and exceeding strategic plan goals.

One of the important roles of a CEO is to have a succession plan in place. If something happens to the CEO, what happens the next day? The plan should include the following:

1. **Organization Structure Review**
   - Management Span/Departments
   - Organization Chart

2. **Position Overview**
   - Job Description
   - Competencies/Expertise Required
   - Skills/Training/Education Requirements
3. **Potential Candidates**
   - Internal and External
   - Strengths and Weaknesses
   - Development Possibilities
   - Time Frame
4. **Resources**
   - Search Firms
   - Industry Lists
   - Industry Magazines/Advertising Opportunities
   - Appropriate Forms of Social Media (i.e., LinkedIn)
5. **Interim Plan**
   - What to Do During the Search
     + Interim CEO
     + Steps and Time Frames
     + Communication Vehicle

It is imperative that the plan is updated and reviewed annually and remains ready to be put into place if necessary.

We all know that no position is 100 percent secure, and sometimes it becomes necessary to part ways with your organization. If that time comes, what's the best way to leave, and how do you tell your board you're leaving? Hopefully, this issue would be dealt with in a timely and healthy manner, leaving time for a successful transition to a new leader. The CEO and board members should have the best interest of the organization at heart and work together about how to end the relationship, inform the constituency, and plan what happens next as it relates to the succession plan. If you are planning to leave the organization, it's helpful to let others know of your intentions to ensure an open dialogue about your decision. It's best for the organization—and you—if there are no surprises. How you exit an organization will speak volumes about who you are and the values you have. Remember, be authentic!

Part 4

BE SUCCESSFUL

My dad always loved sports. He taught us to play baseball and coached our Little League teams. The love of sports my brothers and I have to this day emanates from the wonderful times we had with our father in his official and unofficial capacity as our coach. When we were growing up, Saturdays and Sundays were special days, because we gathered around the television to watch the game of the week. Even as we watched football or baseball games, my father looked for opportunities to teach.

My dad hated touchdown dances, those displays of celebration and vanity that started in the National Football League back in the 1970s. One day we watched a game during which a top NFL running back scored three touchdowns, without outwardly celebrating any of them. When interviewed after the game and asked why he hadn't danced, the running back said that he didn't need to celebrate touchdowns because he wasn't all that surprised he had made them. "Players who celebrate wildly seem very surprised to have scored," he said. On the other hand, he was not surprised to have scored and expected that he would score again. So instead of dancing, he simply handed the ball back to the referee and went back to the game. My dad exclaimed, "Now there is a role model for you!"

The Lesson

The confidence that football player exhibited is a fundamental message of this part of the book. If you expect success and are confident in your abilities, it shouldn't be a big surprise when it occurs. Success shouldn't be overwhelming, because it's expected and you worked hard to achieve it. You made a plan and you believed that it could work. Now you'll learn to achieve your goals and find the high level of success to which you aspire.

You'll need to keep working at becoming a skilled and confident leader, just as the football player works every day to improve his skills. By doing so, you will be successful, and you won't be surprised.

You've read about *wanting* to be a leader, *planning* to be a leader, and *acting* like a leader. In this section, you'll learn how to navigate your way as a leader and find true success.

Chapter 20

I've Met the Enemy and It Is Us!

My dad used to tell us a story about a farmer who had a pasture that bordered the railroad tracks. One day when counting his cattle, the farmer realized that one cow was missing. He went to the train station in town and talked with the local manager of the railroad company. The farmer told the manager he thought the train that passed through town had probably killed one of his cows, because one was missing. He also reported that neither he nor any of his neighbors had heard a train whistle that morning, meaning that the engineer had not whistled to get the cattle off the track, and therefore was at fault for killing his cow.

The manager said he would have the railroad company's lawyer look into the matter and pay a visit to the farmer the next day. The lawyer came out to the farm and proposed that rather than go to court about the missing cow, the railroad company would give the farmer $500 to settle the matter. The farmer agreed to that and upon receiving his check signed a paper saying he would no longer hold the railroad liable.

After the paper was signed and in the lawyer's jacket pocket, the lawyer told the farmer the reason the train hadn't sounded a whistle was because the engineer was paying no attention to the track and the conductor was asleep. Clearly, the lawyer said, the farmer would have received more money had the matter gone to court. The farmer replied that he doubted he could have more money, since the missing cow had simply been on the other side of the tracks and returned home later that day! This story illustrates that while we like to be smart and clever, we often are our own worst enemies.

THE LESSON

An individual can be his or her worst enemy, and so can departments or even an entire organization. Many organizations simply have bad business practices. They don't set out with a goal of cultivating bad business practices; they result from ineffective leadership. Bad business practices are developed and sustained through that hallowed mantra of "we have always done it this way." As you read earlier in the book, Tom Peters once said, "Most quality programs fail for one of two reasons: systems without passion, or passion without systems."

While a sense of passion and compassion is a critical component for an authentic and effective leader, it will not sustain a company that practices bad business. In this and following chapters, you'll read about what should be part of your systems to ensure your organization doesn't fail because you don't have effective business practices in place.

Most people associate audits with the IRS and don't like to think about them, but a business audit is an extremely valuable tool and should be employed any time you are facing a new business situation. A business audit is simply a good look at your organization, or a part of your organization, and gives you a handle on what's going on. Never start a leadership job with a new organization without getting to know the company. When you conduct a business audit, check out the following areas.

1. **Human Resources.** Learn about salary structure, benefits, the review process, educational opportunities, promotion opportunities, retention, statistics, morale, and, perhaps most important, the issues employees experience. Make it a point to visit as many people as you can. While employees are telling you how their departments work, they'll also give you a clear picture of employee morale and other issues you might need to address.

2. **Financial.** Learn about the budgeting process; the types of reports you'll receive; and how purchases, expenses, revenue, and other budget items are reported. Learn how often you will receive reports and what happens if corrective action is

required. Understand how purchases are made, vendors are selected, and who has authority for what. Ask a lot of questions in this area, and be prepared to make suggestions. Organizations often make mistakes, like using antiquated lists of vendors, not using competitive or quantitative purchasing agreements, and generating financial reports that are not meaningful. Often, little corrective action is taken if budgets are out of whack or you haven't received information you need to make effective decisions.

One of the quickest ways you can make an impact is to help streamline and simplify meaningful reports, and to find areas in which you can save money. During my first year as CEO of Caron, we saved more than $200,000 on insurance products. I found out we'd been using the same vendor for more than ten years without putting the contracts out to bid. The price kept increasing and we kept paying the increases until we looked for bids and less expensive contracts. As a CFO friend always says, "It's hard to fill up a bucket when there's a hole at the bottom." Too often, organizations don't do enough to plug the hole.

3. **Roles of Departments and Divisions.** What you will learn will vary, depending on whether a department generates revenue by making a product or distributing or providing a service, or if it's a support group that assists other departments to generate income. Regardless, it's critical to ascertain the role of each department within the overall organization and have a clear understanding of how it fits into the strategic plan. You need a good understanding of the future of the department. Is it

stable, growing, being phased out, or combined with another? Whatever its status, it needs a short-term action plan. Make sure you understand the role and relationship each department has with other departments. Who are the suppliers, and who does the department supply? Know the politics to promote effective relationships.

4. **Culture of the Organization.** You'll need a sense of the culture and the attitudes of individuals. You can better understand the culture of your organization during interactions with team members. Is it paternalistic? Do employees view the organization as a family? Are relationships formal or informal? Also try to ascertain whether or not the culture is consistent. Does everyone view it in the same way? Attitudes can vary dramatically.

Learning about the culture of each department and whether it's consistent with other areas of the organization is helpful as you develop a leadership plan. If you feel the culture is not conducive to the health of the department or the company, you do not need to accept the culture. Before you start trying to change it, however, you need to understand it.

I once worked at a different organization, also a not-for-profit. We hired a senior-level person who had zero experience in a not-for-profit environment. Shortly after his arrival, another executive vice president and I suggested that we take him out to lunch and explain the culture of the organization to him. He said that wasn't necessary, but he appreciated our interest. He may have intellectually grasped some of the areas integral to the organization, but he didn't make any effort to ask questions or engage in them.

About a year later he came to me, complaining and frustrated about the organizational culture. He had been told that his job was to produce specific results and, based on his expertise, tried to make a few changes he felt were necessary to achieve that bottom line. When he tried to make the changes, he was told he couldn't implement them if they were contrary to the mission and philosophy of the organization. As a result, he didn't meet the bottom line and felt he had been attacked for not doing so.

Two years later we terminated the manager. He never did understand the culture, which prevented him from doing his job effectively. Don't underestimate the importance of assessing the culture of your department and organization. If you understand the culture of your organization—but your activities continue to fly in the face of it—you will experience consequences.

5. **Your Staff.** Learn about your team's areas of expertise, how long they've been on board, and their strengths and weaknesses. You'll need to retain your employees when you first arrive, as it's typically very difficult and time-consuming to start replacing people right away. Refer to Chapter 15 on coaching so you can help your staff accomplish the necessary goals when you're first starting out, and remember that an important attribute of a leader is to inspire. You'll need this trait when you take on a new leadership role. When I came to Caron as CEO in 1995,

I found out that the number-two person, the chief operating officer (COO), was planning to leave. He assumed the new CEO would bring in others from his previous organization, so he'd secured another position. I needed him to stay, and doing so was the most important action I undertook in my first thirty days at Caron. I inspired him to help me turn the organization around. Over the next five years, together we were able to accomplish some great results. Assess your staff quickly and determine the roles they'll play in your short-term plan. Once such a plan is in place, you can determine who will be on your team for the long haul.

6. **The Ninety-Day Plan.** Once you have visited with staff and colleagues throughout the organization and have a good understanding of morale, finances, how each department fits into the greater organization, you'll then want to develop a short-term action plan—typically something to be accomplished in ninety days. Based on the information you've gathered, identify steps you can take in the next ninety days to develop momentum.

For people to dream about the future, they first need to have hope. Hope will come as you instill a sense of confidence that you can, and will, achieve success. Having a plan in place and meeting the goals of the plan within the first ninety days lets employees see that you mean what you say and that you're an authentic boss.

To that end, the goals of a ninety-day plan must be achievable as well as clearly identified, measured, and communicated. Make the plan known to all employees, and engage them in working on it with you. This creates a sense of teamwork and camaraderie. I've seen too many people who move into new positions spend too much time studying, analyzing, becoming familiar, and not really doing much. I believe it's far more effective to come in, visit as many folks as possible in the first several weeks, and *then* present an action plan. You will become known as being proactive—a person of action who is results oriented.

Each department should develop critical success factors. Make sure that people understand them and are clear about the tasks that must be accomplished for the plan to be a success. Continually communicate progress and compliment staff when they achieve their goals. During this period, your team will learn your style of communication, method of evaluation, and overall management style. The key is to remain authentic, consistent, and persistent about your important values. At the end of ninety days, you will have established yourself as a leader.

Chapter 21

Empowering Idiots

My dad was a big believer in the importance of common sense. Unfortunately, he often said, "Common sense is not all that common!" He shared with me this story, which highlights that sentiment.

Two farmers whose farms bordered each other did not get along, and there was always a dispute between them, mostly involving the property line. One farmer was tired of all the trouble, so he proposed that he put up a fence and they split the cost. The second farmer wanted nothing to do with a fence or paying for it. Furthermore, he told the first farmer that if any part of the fence was on his land, he'd sue him.

So the first farmer had his land surveyed and built the fence three feet inside the line to make sure there would be no mistake and no part of his fence would be on the other man's property. Upon completing the fence, he went back to the other farmer and told him that the fence was clearly on his side of the property. Any cattle that touched his fence would be trespassing on his property. If that happened, or the cattle in any way damaged the fence, he would sue the other farmer.

The second farmer decided that he couldn't risk that happening, so he, too, built a fence, three feet inside the property line so that no part of his fence would be on the first farmer's property. Now these two farmers had two fences instead of one, and had wasted six feet of valuable farmland along the entire border of their properties. Not a bit of common sense went into their decisions, but they each had their own fence.

THE LESSON

A classic line from an old management movement called Total Quality Management (TQM) says, "If you empower idiots, they will make stupid decisions." A key focus of TQM was empowerment of employees. Managers were supposed to empower employees at all levels so that decisions could be made at the lowest level of the organization. I don't have a problem with empowering employees— I think it's a good practice. However, allowing employees to make decisions they're not equipped to make, or giving them responsibilities they're not prepared to handle, doesn't make any sense. Giving people power without providing the training or skills necessary to utilize that power can be devastating, both to employees and the organization.

The place to start for anyone in a new leadership role is to assemble a team that can be trained to effectively utilize its level of empowerment to make good decisions. Qualities I look for when selecting a team include the following:

+ Loyalty to me and the organization
+ A skill set that matches the position. For example, a CFO must have an accounting or finance background.
+ Passionate about our mission and philosophy
+ Possess leadership qualities (the most desirable attributes are outlined in Appendix B)
+ Comfortable taking on responsibility and being accountable for their decisions
+ A proven track record of success
+ A strong work ethic
+ A commitment to values consistent with the organizational culture and principles
+ Clear understanding of themselves, and the ability to articulate their goals and plans for the future
+ Upbeat, positive, enjoy their work, and do it well.

When setting up a team, look for people who have different types of information-processing skills. You don't need five people who process information exactly like you do; you'll wind up with five individuals who always come up with the same answer. At Caron, we work with consultants on executive assessment. This is an important part of interviewing for key positions, as it helps to see the individual's leadership style and how it might fit in with or balance the current team.

The external consultant helps us understand how we will work together as a team and what our challenges might be. This goes a long way toward building sound relationships as a team and getting to know one another better. It also prepares team members for conflicts that could arise, teaching them how to deal with it if it does. This process is valuable for new teams, but it's also useful for a team that has been in place for a while. A 360-degree review is an excellent technique for a leadership team, for it highlights each member's strengths, identifies weaknesses, and, with a facilitator, develops a plan to work even more effectively together.

Great organizations are continually learning. It's important to provide ongoing training for your staff, for it pays in the long run. The training might be technical, or can be more general in nature, highlighting topics of critical importance, such as leadership and motivation. I believe, in fact, that most organizations need to provide more training to help employees become better leaders. This type of training should be ongoing. Training costs money, and many companies cut it when looking for financial savings.

While it can be painful, it is essential to eliminate team members who don't fit. A team member who doesn't pull his or her weight, doesn't have the right chemistry, or lacks a key ingredient such as loyalty or passion can drag down the rest of the team. You do yourself, the individual, and your team a great service when you terminate an individual who is clearly not a part of the team. It also sends a powerful message to others about your ability to be decisive. Firing a team member is difficult. Let's take a look at why it's so hard and how to do it when it's necessary.

One of the most uncomfortable and unpleasant tasks of being a leader is terminating an employee. I hate it. However, as I've told a number of individuals whom I've had to terminate, the good of the organization is the highest priority. If they're not contributing to the organization, they don't belong at Caron.

If you haven't had much experience with terminating employees, you need to learn a lot before doing so. There is a lot of information available (even seminars) that addresses many important elements to understand about termination. These include the importance of human resource documentation, legal considerations regarding how to present the information to the employee, making sure the employee has had an opportunity to address whatever the situation might be, putting together an appropriate package that might involve outplacement services and severance. The message is this: if you have not done a termination, get the expert assistance of a human-resource professional, a human-resource consultant, or legal counsel.

The reason for discussing termination in this chapter stems from the fact that you can't effectively build your team if you don't have the right players. As you develop your plan for the future, you may assess your current talent pool and realize that three out of five positions don't fit. If that's the case, develop a plan to replace those positions over a period of time.

When I came to Caron, one of my biggest goals was to dramatically improve the financial performance of the organization. This was accomplished without eliminating any staff during my first two years as president. Once we returned the institution to financial stability, I then developed a plan to move some staff out and bring others in who could help us move to the next level. I could not have replaced all of them initially, but by developing a time frame, I was able to move several of them out in a manner that was beneficial to them as well as the organization. Take a long-term view at what your team needs to look like, and keep in mind that as your organization grows and changes, the team you have today may not be the team you will need in the future. Continually look for ways to improve your team.

When interviewing someone for a spot on your team, keep in mind some considerations. First, consult your organization's human resource department about rules pertaining to the interview process, what questions you should or shouldn't ask. That's really important. I'll share a few I feel are very important during the interview process.

You already know that I think a personality test is a must, so have a corporate psychologist or human resource agency do that. Ask questions about values, career plans, and priorities in life. Ask questions that allow you to see how the person you're interviewing thinks. Try to find teammates who share similar values and a passion for your particular cause. Values can be developed, but it's easier to recruit people who already have them.

Since I've spent the bulk of my life in a not-for-profit workforce, I need to say something about teammates in a not-for-profit environment. There's always been a perception that individuals in not-for-profit fields are paid less, and somehow they don't need to be as talented as people in a for-profit field. This perception also assumes that not as much should be expected from not-for-profit workers, that somehow they couldn't make it in the "real" corporate world. I'd like to put these misconceptions to rest.

If an employee can make more money elsewhere and that's an important value for that person, he or she should go for it. However, most not-for-profits have been working to increase their pay schedules to be competitive with for-profit companies. Most people work for not-for-profits because they're committed to the cause of the organization, but they still expect—and deserve—adequate compensation. Good organizations learn to develop fair compensation practices so that they attract top-rate, talented individuals. Not-for-profits do not want a reputation for hiring less-talented individuals. We would be empowering idiots, a move that is totally unacceptable for any business.

Chapter 22

Get on the Train

The story went that a neighbor from a nearby farm decided to teach his smartest pig to sing. The pig was clever not to question this goal, and the farmer was convinced that he could make the pig's squeal sound like a song. The farmer thought this would be a wonderful trick. He'd enter the pig in the county fair, the state fair, and who knew how successful they could be? He had the idea that everyone would want to hear his pig sing, and he could make a great fortune from the venture.

So he worked diligently to coach the pig to sing by singing to the pig. He rewarded the pig when it seemed to cooperate, which, truth be told, wasn't very often. This went on for weeks, and everyone waited to see if he would be successful. One day the farmer went into town, and everybody he saw wanted to know if his pig was singing. The farmer had to admit defeat. The pig would not sing. Additionally, the farmer said, the pig had been acting very strange and unco-operative—probably a result of all those singing lessons!

The moral of this story, of course, is that you can't make a pig sing (or fly!). Just as the farmer realized that he would typically irritate and annoy the pig while trying to make it sing, so, too, in business some employees are like the pig. You cannot make them sing, they won't learn how to sing, and you will annoy them when trying to make them sing!

THE LESSON

For a workforce to be effective, everybody needs to be moving in the same direction. The entire team needs to be working off the same plan, with everyone striving toward the same goal. When I became president at Caron, I spent thirty days taking an inventory and assessing the situation. After that, I presented a ninety-day plan for the organization, which was followed by a strategic plan for the next three years.

While presenting the ninety-day plan, I used the analogy of "getting on the train." The plan spelled out my expectations so that every employee knew what they were. The plan clearly showed where we were going and how we were going to get there. Each employee knew where he or she fit into the plan, and I invited them all to "get on the train." Employees would have thirty days to decide if they were going to accept the invitation. If they showed up in thirty days, that was their pledge that they were coming along for the ride.

Basically, employees had three responses to the new plan. Two of them put them on the train, and one of them did not. Employees who agreed with the plan and accepted it were on the train. So were those who didn't agree with the plan but would accept it and abide by it. The third group (these are like the pigs whom you can't make sing), those who didn't agree and wouldn't accept the plan, were urged to exercise their exit visas. Some employees chose the third option, and we helped them to find employment elsewhere. Remember, just like you can't make pigs sing, it's critical to determine the employees who can't get on the train. Not only will they not be able to get on the train, they will also be annoyed and irritated as well.

When you're new to a situation or in a new leadership role, having the support of your staff is critical. Team members have to support you and your plan. So asking everyone to pledge their support becomes more than symbolic; it helps employees think through the roles they will play within the organization. A previous employer of mine asked everyone to sign the strategic plan. We had a ceremony where a huge copy of the plan was displayed and everyone signed it. It was very symbolic, but it also made all of us ask the question of whether or not we wanted to be part of something. Signing the plan invested us in it and increased our commitment to seeing it through.

Once the train is headed down the track, keep employees informed of its progress. They need to know how fast the train is moving, if the train is still on the track, or if the train has stopped at the station. During the early days of leadership, it's key to keep team members updated on how you're doing. Keep the information simple, and communicate it in a meaningful way so that everyone feels included and can understand what's happening. And communicate consistently as you move through the plan.

You read earlier about the importance of including some easily reached markers in the ninety-day plan. This enables you to show results early on, and to build a level of confidence in your leadership and faith in your ability to produce the results you promised. Achieving these early results also helps employees to believe in their ability to perform. They start to see that when plans are carefully thought out and implemented, they will move forward. This creates the kind of hope and hopefulness that ultimately allows an organization to develop a powerful vision for the future. Nothing breeds success like success!

Once your team members are on the train, be prepared to make some stops at the station. Not everybody will stay on the train for the long haul, so be prepared to let some employees get off and bring others on. Make sure new riders understand the importance of being fully on board. Note that employee input and debate is encouraged during the planning process. Should a particular plan not meet its goals, employee input is urged. This is different from "criticizing the plan." Input for development and corrective action is necessary. We work diligently in helping our employees understand the difference.

At Caron, employees are readily forgiven for mistakes made when they "sin boldly" on behalf of a program or patient they're trying to move forward. Bad attitudes and critical natures toward our long-range plans and mission, however, are not tolerated. Negativity can spread through an organization like a cancer, and it's not tolerated under my watch. Employees who can't be positive are directed to the human resource department. If they can't adjust their attitudes and get on the train, they can utilize their exit visas. The key to being successful is including everybody on one train, heading in the same direction, with a capable crew that knows where it's going.

Chapter 23

Hopefully, the Customer Is Always the Customer

A single mother in town had a full-time job and was raising her six-year-old daughter the very best she could. She balanced spending time with her child and taking care of the household with her full-time employment. Her time was a valuable commodity, and managing it well was imperative. Her little daughter fell in love with the story of Cinderella and asked her mother to read it to her every night. After reading it over and over and over, the harried mother had the idea to record her voice reading the story and give the recording to her daughter to listen to whenever she wanted. She explained to the little girl how the recorder worked and had her practice pressing the buttons and using the device.

The little girl listened to the story for a while on the recorder, but before long came to her mom and asked her if she would read the Cinderella book to her. The tired mother, who was catching up on bills, asked with a bit of exasperation if there was a problem with the recorder. The little girl said the recorder was fine except for one thing. "It doesn't have a lap, Mommy."

THE LESSON

What a message that story sends about the importance of the human touch, personal relationships, and connectedness. It wasn't the Cinderella tale that was important to the six-year-old; it was being close to her mother. It's an important message for everyone, as it speaks to all our relationships—families, friends, colleagues, and even our clients and customers.

Chapter 12 explored the issue of knowing where your heart is and caring deeply about whatever you do. If you produce a product or provide a service, you should care about what you're offering. You should care about it because you're handing it over to your customers. Whatever that product or service is, the reason your organization and you are there is to serve your customers or clients. We all get bogged down with meetings, paperwork, and strategic planning, and it's sometimes easy to lose sight of the customer. However, as a leader, you can take a number of actions to help you and your team members maintain a customer focus.

Your customer, whether another business, an individual, a patient, or whatever, must always come first. Conflicts that arise within the workplace should always be resolved by thinking about what's best for the customer. A manager once came to me and asked if I would support her concerning a disagreement between her and several of her direct reports about the way a program was being run. I informed her that my commitment was to our patients. I wouldn't be taking the side of management or subordinates. I would take the side of the patient, who would benefit from the disputed program and look for the resolution that provided for the patient's best care.

Any time a disagreement arises between staff members, either in the same department or between departments, a simple way to put them back on track is to ask, "What is most effective for our patient?" Once we're united behind a common goal of serving our patients in the very best manner possible, it becomes a whole lot easier to develop a strategy.

I worked at an organization where I became involved in a debate about scheduling staff over the weekend. A director of a program felt that the weekend program at the organization was weak, since the vast majority of premier staff members worked Monday to Friday. Because they had seniority, they felt they had earned the right to work "normal hours." Newly hired, part-time, and lesser degreed employees usually were scheduled for second and third shifts, as well as weekends.

However, as quality reports began to show that our customers were concerned about the drop-off in our program's quality over the weekends, the executive director correctly decided that something needed to be done to improve weekend treatment. He called all staff together on a Friday and asked for input. Then he worked for an entire weekend to develop a schedule. The executive director was proud of his proposal, and he called his staff back together on Monday to share it with them. He revealed the plan, expecting accolades and congratulations for the hard work he'd invested in putting together a complex schedule. However, he had considered very little of the input the staff had offered that previous Friday, including that many did not want to work on the weekends. In his new schedule, the majority of his staff would now be working some weekends. Hence, the staff received the plan with a great deal of criticism, anger, frustration, and even threats of resignation.

Looking for resolution, employees on both sides of the weekend issue showed up at my office later that day. As we started hashing it out, I made sure they all understood that the executive director had the V, and it was ultimately his decision. We agreed that everyone whose lives would be impacted by the changes should be directly involved in the decision. It was apparent that the input of those employees had not been effectively utilized. I asked them to describe weekend treatment, and all employees on both sides of the issue agreed that it was not as good as weekday treatment. I asked team members if they felt committed to bringing the level of care up to par with weekday treatment. Long-term employees acknowledged that they needed to be involved over the weekend to improve the quality of care offered. They agreed to develop among themselves a schedule that would have them all work the same number of weekend days over a month. While they were committed to providing better care for patients over the weekend, they didn't want to be scheduled without having their input considered. By coming up with a schedule on their own, they were able to figure out who preferred to work Saturdays, Sundays, overnights, consecutive days, etc. The issue of patient care became the driving force in rescheduling employees. Involving those concerned and underscoring their commitment made it a lot easier to get the job done.

The question of whether you're putting your patient or customer first must be foremost in every decision you make. If the matter at hand doesn't concern or have any impact on the customer or patient, I challenge you to think about why you're even spending time on it. Dick Caron, who founded Caron Treatment Centers in 1957, employed a basic approach to decision making. A motto he frequently repeated was, "Remember, it's about the patient, dummy!" In its simplicity, the motto was a constant reminder to Caron's early staff to work toward better treatments and programs and do an even better job for the individuals they were serving.

Unfortunately, as organizations grow and employees become further removed from the customer, there's a tendency not to keep customers in the forefront of the company's mission. I have a friend who leads a large healthcare organization and has increasingly isolated himself in his executive suite. I tease him that he wouldn't know what a patient looked like if he tripped over one, but I really think it's quite sad. I'm fortunate to work for an organization that believes it's important for the CEO to have a presence on our campuses and among our patients, and I make sure other executives have that interaction as well. We eat in the same dining hall as patients, talk to them, visit with their families, sit down with referents, and make sure our customers know who we are. I even do a monthly lecture to our patients—I want them to know who the CEO is! It's rare for the CEO of a large treatment center to have this type of patient interaction. Our patients tell us they like that caring starts at the very top of the organization. Regardless of the type of service or product you provide, it's important that management develops strategies to make sure everyone knows who the customers are and interacts with them appropriately.

Every chance I get, I remind staff to stay patient centered. Caron has grown dramatically in the past decade, and I recognize the possibility exists that we could lose some of our passion for our patients as we tend to capital expansion and program improvements. However, what we do is not about growing the organization or minding our egos, it's, in the words of our founder, "about the patient, dummy!" We will continue to be driven by that goal, as it is always about the patient and "Recovery is our only bottom line."

Chapter 24

Good Ain't Good Enough Anymore

I absolutely loved sports when I was young, particularly baseball. We had a small yard in front of our house, and my brothers and I laid out our own baseball field in it. It couldn't have been more than fifty feet from home plate to the house, but when we first started playing in the yard, hardly anything we hit went that far. In the early days, our rule was if the ball hit the house, it was a double, and if it landed on the roof, it was a home run.

We improved as we played more, and we were proud when the balls started reaching the house with some regularity. Our parents, however, didn't find that as exciting as we did. So we moved our ballpark to the area in front of the barn. We had a lot more room there, and it was probably 150 to 200 feet from home plate to the grain bins. Similar to our earlier rules, a ball hit to the bin was considered a double. If a ball went over the bins, it was a home run. As we became older and better players, we started losing a fair number of balls we hit over the bins and out on to the road.

Our father suggested we move to the pasture, where he helped us lay out an even bigger ballpark with a distance of about 300 feet between home plate and the creek. Our hits rarely reached the creek when we first moved to the new field, but after a while we had to put up a fence to keep balls from rolling into the water. Over a period of years, as we grew older, stronger, and more proficient at playing baseball, we outgrew all our playing fields, from the front yard, to the area in front of the barn, and finally the pasture. What was considered a good hit in the front yard would have been a modest hit in front of the barn and insignificant in the pasture. As we grew up and became better at baseball, more and more was expected from us if we were to be considered good players. The same concept holds true in the workplace.

THE LESSON

A great quote from Bill Wilson, the founder of Alcoholics Anonymous, summarizes this evolution beautifully: "The good or seemingly good is oftentimes the fatal enemy of the perpetual best." I take that to mean that getting too comfortable with doing something reasonably well can lead to a level of complacency that leaves you in the dust. The rules of competition suggest that an organization continues to improve, or the period of comfortableness it has reached will be followed by failure.

If you're reading this book, regardless of your position in your company, you are probably driven to higher levels of performance. The question is, how do you motivate your staff to adopt the same attitude?

Caron was struggling financially when I arrived in 1995. In two years, we had turned the situation around and were on our way back. As management continued to look for areas in which we could improve, some staff members questioned why we were working so hard to bring about improvements when things seemed to be going so well. The organization was back on the right path, so why would we need to do more, or take more risk and create challenges that required the attention of all employees?

Over time I was able to convince staff that good ain't good enough anymore, but it's taken a lot of reminding over the years to keep everyone on board. Continued and sustained improvement is not always a universal philosophy. It might be how you do business, but you likely have employees who balk at the thought. Unless you permeate this philosophy and make it part of your staff's culture, you will have real difficulty in continuing to increase your organization's performance. Continually raise the bar and encourage team members to follow.

Implementing continuous improvement initiatives means your organization has to always develop the culture. That is, always thinking about how to move forward. Empowering staff to make decisions that improve the service or the product, having teams that continually look for better ways of doing things, measuring customer service and efficiency, and utilizing data to make improvements are business techniques that, once in place, will help your organization to keep improving.

Also vital to continuous improvement are effective meetings and follow-ups to minimize waste of time, as well as having measurements in place to evaluate customer service, cost effectiveness, and all financial enterprises. Those measurements can provide meaningful data that can direct you on how to improve as an organization. I once had a president who claimed that if you weren't always getting better, you were, effectively, getting worse. No organization wants that as its goal, and that's why it's so important to create and sustain a culture that features a commitment to growing, improving, and being more efficient in measurable ways.

In health care, every patient doesn't "get well." But our company culture tells us that our job is to try, all the time, to help increasing numbers of patients achieve wellness in recovery. We have developed tools to better understand our success rate, and every year we invest in new strategies based on research that direct us on how we can improve that success rate. If we increase our success rate by just 1 percent, that means ten more people out of every 1,000 we treat "get well."

Regardless of what industry you're a part of, you'll need to implement simple, understandable measures with which your staff can identify. Communicate those measures often so that you can create a culture in which everyone is looking for ways to improve. That will create an environment where everyone realizes that good ain't good enough anymore.

Chapter 25

The Trump Card—
Use It!

When I was in grade school, we were expected to sell Christmas cards each year. The school told students how many boxes we were each expected to sell, and we went door to door in town and to our farm neighbors, asking them to buy cards from us. One year the school brought in a representative from the company that distributed the Christmas cards to give us tips on how to sell as many boxes as we could.

He said that one successful technique was when a woman answered the door, he inquired as to whether or not her parents were home. The lady of the house would blush and feel good about her youthful look. This flattery would typically result in a generous Christmas card purchase.

I made a mental note of this seemingly easy technique as I set off for my first house. A lady answered the door, and I cheerfully said, "Good evening, Miss. Are your parents home?"

Clearly confounded, she responded, "Are you crazy? They're ninety years old and in a rest home, so you can go see them there if you'd like!"

Needless to say, I didn't get the sale. What I failed to understand from the sales rep was that my engagement with a potential consumer should be appropriately tailored. In other words, saying something nice to somebody if it's totally unsuitable is not effective or meaningful.

✦ ✦ ✦

A priest woke up early on a Sunday morning and decided to play a quick nine holes at a local golf course. He figured the early start would allow him enough time to get through the front nine and still make it back to say Mass. He hurriedly packed up his clubs and set off for the golf course.

Meanwhile, Saint Peter and God were watching from heaven. God said he thought the priest needed a reminder about what his priorities should be for a Sunday morning and advised Saint Peter to watch what God would do.

The priest stepped up to the first hole and made a terrific drive, resulting in a birdie. The second hole was another birdie and the third hole an eagle. The priest was excited, as this was the best golf he'd ever played. He finished the nine holes with his best score ever.

So now he had a decision to make. He could pack up and head to Mass, or see if his luck continued on the back nine. Just too tempted by his great success, he gave in and continued playing. The priest completed the round with a staggering fifteen holes under par—a course record—but he missed his church service!

Saint Peter had been watching all this and didn't understand how God was supposedly reminding the priest that his time on Sunday morning would best be spent in church and not on the golf course. When he asked, God chuckled and said, "He played the best golf of his life, but who's he going to tell?"

Great accomplishments can seem like hollow achievements if they can't be shared, acknowledged, and celebrated.

THE LESSON

Meaningful praise, sharing achievements, can be the trump card you need. When the going gets tough, you need a trump card. A manager must have a tool when it seems like nothing else is working. Fortunately, your trump card is within easy reach. It doesn't cost a thing to use, and it's very effective: meaningful praise for an achievement.

One study after another has shown that employees respond to achievement and recognition. Nearly everyone likes to feel like they've accomplished something important and wants to be recognized for that achievement. As a recent study by California-based Bersin & Associates revealed, a little recognition can go a long way.

The 2012 study showed that companies with recognition programs that improve employee engagement have 31-percent lower voluntary turnover than companies with no such programs. These companies also had high-performing employees and positive work environments. The recognitions, the study showed, didn't need to be elaborate or expensive. Something as easy as recognizing an employee's accomplishment on the company blog proved helpful.[2]

Every company has the potential to employ recognition and meaningful praise, but it all starts with you, the boss. As the priest supposedly learned, achievement without recognition isn't all that satisfactory. In a perfect world, we'd all strive to achieve as a result of self-motivation and because it's the right thing to do; but let's face it, we all like to be recognized for our accomplishments.

A good leader coaches team members so they're able to meet goals and experience a sense of achievement. And then that leader recognizes team members for what they've done. This sounds like such an easy and simple strategy, but often it's underused or not used at all. Managers spend so much time on meetings, phone calls, e-mails, problem solving, and basically just being busy that we don't take time to tell our team members we appreciate what they've done

---

2 See *http://marketing.bersin.com/rs/bersin/images/060812_MB_RecognitionBenchmarking_SSG_Final.pdf*.

and how their efforts truly matter. Making recognition a part of the culture of your organization takes practice and persistence; it must become a habit you employ on a regular basis. Like any other habit, it takes time to make it seem like a natural part of your business routine.

When I started running again after having taken some time off, I didn't start out at ten miles a day. I started at a mile or two and kept a record of how far and fast I'd run on any given day. That way I could see the patterns of when I ran, when I skipped, my distance, and my times. If I missed two or three days in a row, I had to step up my plan. As my times and endurance improved, it was time to add distance. Before long I was in the habit of running, and it became part of my daily routine.

Employee recognition works the same way. Start by expressing recognition to one employee every day, and make a note when you do it. You'll be able to chart your progress, and after a few weeks it will have become a habit. There may be days when you don't find opportunity for recognition, but on most days you will. Recognizing and affirming employees with meaningful praise is one of the easiest techniques you can do. It's also one of the most effective.

Meaningful praise, however, has to be just that: meaningful. Employees will sense immediately if you are not sincere. As you've read many times already, they want you to be authentic. Also, be as specific as you can. Instead of saying something generic like, "Sarah, that sure was a good job," spell out the act you are recognizing. Your words will have a lot more impact if you say, "Sarah, staying late yesterday and helping that patient through a very difficult situation had a powerful impact and meant a lot to her and other patients, too. I'm really proud of what you did and want to thank you for it." With those words, you let Sarah know that you're aware of the situation and you recognize that she did the right thing.

Sharing praise also is a powerful form of recognition. One of the real treasures in my job is when I receive an e-mail or the occasional letter from a grateful patient or family member about the specific work of an employee. I always make sure to share those words with the staff member and his or her supervisors. It's nice for the employee to receive the recognition, but it's an extra "warm fuzzy," as one of my team members says, to know that the boss is aware of it and cared enough to share it with the employee.

Don't limit meaningful praise to just lower- or middle-level employees, but offer it to your peers and supervisors, as well. As you climb the ladder within an organization, you may start to feel like you're competing with other employees who are at the same level. It can seem like you're all working toward fewer senior-level positions, and your tendency might be to pull back from your peers and not offer recognition of their accomplishments.

Knowing that I had higher aspirations for my career, a wise board member once gave me a piece of valuable advice. Rather than viewing my peers as competitors, the board member said I should look at them as colleagues who could help me move to the next level. The more I collaborated and helped, cooperated and praised, the more they reciprocated—and we all benefited. Recognizing your peers in a genuine manner goes a long way toward encouraging and motivating them to help you to be successful.

Offering praise to a supervisor also is appropriate and will be appreciated. And when offered genuinely, it can make superiors take note that you appreciate their efforts and commitment to the organization.

While you'll have many opportunities for employee recognition during the normal course of work, ideal opportunities exist outside the course of the normal day. The annual review, which we discussed in Chapter 19, is one of those times. It's certainly appropriate to incorporate recognition and meaningful praise into the annual review if it is deserved. An annual review gives you opportunity to discuss with team members what they are doing well and to point out areas that need improvement. Use the review as a teaching moment and talk about an employee's career aspirations within the organization.

With that information, you can identify ways for the employee to grow and move ahead, such as attending conferences, taking classes, or participating in other activities to improve skills. Let the employee know that you are interested and invested in his or her growth. This type of commitment from a supervisor toward staff members breeds commitment and loyalty. Your team members will go the extra mile to perform because they know you are behind them.

To this point, we have talked about utilizing praise and compliments when the opportunity presents itself. I encourage you to find those opportunities. There are times—the annual performance review, for instance—when every organization requires you to spend time with your subordinates and review their performance, which obviously provides an opportunity to offer meaningful praise. In

Chapter 19, we discussed how you should approach the performance review when you are being evaluated. Basically, it is reversed when you are conducting the review. Remember to always make this a meaningful experience by adhering to the following:

1. **Do it in a timely way.** Too many supervisors "get busy" and do not get the reviews done within the appropriate time frame. It sends a negative message to staff members when their annual review date comes and goes and their supervisor didn't find the time to spend with them to do it "on time." But, first and foremost, make sure you schedule the review well in advance and within the appropriate time. This sends a message to the employee that this important and you want to do it in a timely manner.

2. **Make sure to allot enough time for the review.** You do not want it to be rushed. You don't want to get two-thirds of the way through it, look at your watch, and then say, "I've got to go," as you hustle your employee out the door. While conducting reviews, do not take phone calls from customers or allow any other type of interruption, which sends an incredibly negative message. This is sacred time for you and your employee.

3. **Prepare well in advance.** Whatever format you use, make certain to devote thoughtful time, in advance, and complete all sections. Also make sure to make meaningful responses and provide data as appropriate. Stay away from clichés, and give employees concrete examples of their work efforts.

4. **Positively point out areas for improvement.** This is a wonderful time to praise employees for work well done, as well as identify those areas that need development. Point out that this is a teaching moment to identify areas for them to do an even more effective job in the future. Because you care about them, you want to help them in a number of critical places. This is a great time to talk about their careers, what they hope to accomplish within your organization, and to identify growth areas for them to continue on their career tracks. Discuss potential classes, conferences, and other activities for them to improve their skills. This is a great opportunity for them to see you as an investor or participant in their career development. While you are not their mentor, you can certainly be seen as a partner and someone who wants to help them succeed. When staff sees this type of commitment from their supervisor, they become very loyal and will go the extra mile to perform, because they know that you have faith in them, and they want to continue to seek your approval.

5. **Set a schedule for ongoing follow-up.** Too often we conduct the review, point out a handful of things for improvement, send it off to human resources, and then look at it next year; and maybe, if we are lucky, the employee indeed developed some of those growth areas. I make a copy of the areas for improvement, and when I meet with staff members, on a quarterly basis at minimum, I talk about how they're doing with the improvement areas. Just like any other self-improvement area—remember the jogging example—if we don't stay

on top of it and continue to monitor the progress, we'll find that eventually it is forgotten and we don't have a personal or career development plan at all. Do your staff a huge favor and, at least quarterly, discuss how they're progressing on those plans. Again, this demonstrates your care in their development and your interest in seeing them improve. By helping them achieve and effectively recognizing their development, you'll have some very motivated employees.

As mentioned earlier, I believe annual reviews are too infrequent, and even if that is your corporate policy, I suggest you do something semiannually or quarterly. My preference is quarterly, because if things are going well, you have an opportunity to provide praise and motivation as well as monitor professional and career development. If things are status quo or not meeting expectations, it prevents any problems from developing because you can intervene early. At work it seems as though things take on a certain momentum; when things are going well, you want to keep that positive momentum moving forward. By the same token, if something takes on a negative momentum, unless there is an intervention, very often the situation gets worse. A quarterly review helps you intercede and, hopefully, change the negative momentum before it picks up too much speed and you are unable to move it in a positive direction.

Providing praise is a wonderful trump card. Unlike a card game, where you have only so many to play, in the game of business you have many to play. Use them often, because they will indeed help you be successful.

With practice, meaningful praise will come to you easily and others will recognize it as part of your style. When you strive toward being compassionate and offering consistent recognition, you will become known as a leader who genuinely appreciates the work of your employees.

Chapter 26

When to Celebrate

I always enjoyed bucking hay. There's something about being outside on a hot summer day, surrounded by the smell of freshly mowed hay, that gives you a good feeling. It's hard work, to be sure, but you feel a lot of satisfaction when you see a barn fill up with the hay you've bucked.

On the days when the sun beat down and the thermometer rose steadily, my father would remind us how to stay well in the heat. He advised us to drink a lot of water, but in small amounts and not overly cold. "Don't pour water over your head, no matter how hot you are. But pour cool water on your wrists." And he warned us never to gulp large quantities of cold, sugary drinks when really hot, because that could make us sick.

At the end of the day, however, when the hay was in the barn and the air was starting to cool a bit, we celebrated with big glasses of lemonade my mother made. That treat, along with a good dinner and good company, made all the work of the day worth it and left us with a sense of fulfillment and reward.

The town folk who came out to help with bucking often brought cold sugary drinks with them, and my brothers and I sometimes felt envious as they chugged them during work hours. However, having seen more than one of them get sick from those drinks provided a good example of my dad's message to do the work first and enjoy a much better celebration afterward.

THE LESSON

When you experience a milestone or victory at work, you should celebrate. Celebrations mark achievements and keep employees motivated and invested. Instead of waiting until the end of a three-year plan for a celebration, rejoice in the milestones you achieve along the way. Mark big accomplishments like the opening of a new building or reaching a big fund-raising goal, as well as lesser—but still significant—steps like closing a sale or meeting a deadline.

The way you celebrate is based on the culture of your organization—it can be as simple as buying pizza for your staff. You might have a program that provides a bonus check, prizes, or awards, and that's great, too. It's not what you do; it's just the matter of doing it. Celebrations reinforce to your staff that they have been successful, and they should be commensurate with achievement. But be mindful that it's not overdone, because that would be like a running back who celebrates a touchdown with an over-the-top dance. You simply want to acknowledge that your team was successful, offer collective praise, and build expectation that the team will continue to be successful.

Employees like and appreciate celebrations, but heed this warning: if you start them, be prepared to continue them. If you decide to do a quarterly pizza party, for instance, and then after three or four times decide it isn't worth the effort, you will have a lot of unhappy employees. In that case, you'd need to find another way to honor their achievements. Again, employees look for and admire consistency and persistence. Displaying appreciation for their efforts for a while and then tiring of it and stopping is demoralizing and hurtful to staff members, who will wonder if you ever really cared in the first place. The importance of a celebration is that it encourages camaraderie, builds a sense of team, and puts into place the expectation for continued success.

Remember that achievement is rated as the most important factor in employee success. A meaningful celebration is a great way to motivate the team to want to achieve again and again. Take some time to think about reasons you should be celebrating, when it is appropriate to celebrate, and what kinds of celebrations would work for your team or organization. Your employees will thank you for it.

Chapter 27

Pride Is Not a Sin When . . .

My family and I were preparing to make the long drive from Minnesota to Pennsylvania, where we were moving for my new position as CEO and president of Caron Treatment Centers. My wife wanted to detour by her hometown, which is about forty miles west of the Twin Cities. She wanted to say good-bye to a few family members and friends before we began the 1,000-mile drive to our new home.

The town is in a rural area, and there were still some old-fashioned gas stations that didn't offer self-service pumps; full service was the only way to go. The gas gauge on our van was nearing empty when we pulled in and I asked the attendant to fill it up. It would take a little while to dispense thirty gallons of gas, so we settled in to wait. I expected the attendant to check the oil and clean the windows, as is customary with full service, but after he pumped the fuel, he moved around to the passenger side of the van and began chatting with my wife.

They talked and laughed together quietly the entire time the gas was pumping—and then some. It seemed to be quite a spirited conversation, and I was rather baffled as to what was going on. Finally, the attendant replaced the gas cap then handed me back my credit card. I started the engine but had to wait to pull out because the attendant had again gone to the passenger side, this time to say good-bye to my wife. They finished their conversation and off we went.

When I asked my wife who she'd been talking to, she informed me that he was her date to the junior high school prom and her first love. She said she'd really enjoyed talking and reminiscing with him during the short time we were at the gas station. By this time, I was feeling just a little bit of male jealousy and pride. I suggested that it was a good thing I had come along so she could be married to the president of a well-respected organization. "Otherwise, you might be married to a gas station attendant."

She pierced me with a look. "It was clearly *your* good fortune that *I* had come along. Otherwise, maybe you'd be pumping gas and he would be the president!"

THE LESSON

My wife taught me a lesson about self-pride that day. It took me back to Sunday school, where we learned about the seven deadly sins—one of which is pride.

I have learned that self-pride—pride in yourself and what you have done—can lead to arrogance. Arrogance and conceit are crippling attributes for an effective leader. Individuals with these attributes have real difficulty generating passion and compassion, or dispensing genuine and authentic praise. They typically are not inspiring or motivating to their colleagues, as they're too wrapped up in themselves. A confident person has the ability to inspire and motivate, but an arrogant person is a turn-off.

The point is, many arrogant people aren't aware of arrogance in themselves. Sometimes there is a fine line between being confident about your abilities and competencies, and being arrogant. If you tend toward being overly confident in yourself, it might be beneficial to ask trusted colleagues within your organization if they think you are arrogant.

I encourage your organization to use a 360-degree type of review, which is an opportunity for a group of coworkers to provide feedback on an employee's performance. It's an effective tool for determining shortcomings you may have, as well as informing you of your strengths. If part of the feedback you receive is that you are arrogant, work toward eliminating this from your list of character traits.

I've found that an effective strategy to help dispel arrogance is to use a form of self-deprecating humor. Individuals who are comfortable with themselves and their abilities don't feel the need to be prideful or arrogant. Using self-deprecating humor and intentionally knocking yourself down a few pegs makes you more approachable and genuine; someone the rest of your colleagues can relate to. Your insightful colleagues, however, will understand that you do this because you have an inner self-confidence and don't need to tell people how good you are. That helps everyone to be more comfortable.

I once had a long conversation with a gentleman who had retired as chairman of a Fortune 500 company where he had been the president. He was a terrific person with a great sense of humor, much of it at his own expense. In our conversation he told me that he noticed with every move up a level within the organization, he took control over departments he knew very little about. "As I progressed up the ladder, I knew less about more things, until eventually I became president and knew absolutely nothing about everything."

When I became president at Caron, I borrowed that line when introducing myself to employees. I told that story and said, "I hope you're aware that the definition of a president is someone who knows absolutely nothing about everything. Obviously, that's why I was hired." I know they were aware that wasn't true, but it always got a laugh and established a comfort level between us. They saw I wasn't some kind of hotshot who was overly impressed with himself, but that I was a real person with flaws and limitations like everyone else.

I am confident enough in my abilities that I don't need to tell people how good I am. I would rather allow my performance to speak for itself. So I encourage anyone who wants to be a leader to be humble, critical of yourself in a humorous way, and let your actions and abilities speak for themselves. I don't necessarily believe that pride is a sin, but it's certainly an undesirable characteristic.

Pride is *definitely not* a sin when you express it in the accomplishments of your department or your organization. It's important for your colleagues to hear the words *pride* and *proud* often and for them to share your pride in their work. If you make a good product, be proud of that product. If you offer an important service well, be proud of that service. That's the type of pride you should strive for as a leader. Pride in the product or service you provide should be part of the culture of your organization.

When I speak at a function within the field of addiction treatment, I will often mention how proud I am to work in an arena with such dedicated and talented individuals (many of whom are in the audience). When I talk to staff members, I tell them how proud I am to be able to count them as colleagues and to be able to represent the work they do around the country. I share with my direct reports my pride in what they have accomplished and, when presenting to my board, I let them know how proud I am to continue to serve as their ambassador and represent their organization. I express pride in the accomplishments of the staff, pride in board members for the tough choices they make and for their vision in improving the organization.

Nearly everyone enjoys knowing that someone who is important to them feels pride in them. It's important and affirming to know that someone is proud of you, whether it is a parent, a child, a special coach, or a teacher. This is the type of pride you want to share with your colleagues in a significant and a meaningful exchange. Share this type of pride and avoid at all costs being proud of yourself. Pride in your colleagues and the work they perform is positive and powerful, while arrogance and conceit are not.

Chapter 28

Give Until
It Feels Good

I remember a story our pastor told more than thirty years ago on a stewardship Sunday at my church. For the uninitiated, that's the Sunday when the sermon is about the value of giving back to the Lord by giving to the church. There's talk about gifts and tithing, and then congregants turn in their pledge cards, committing to what they'll give that year.

The pastor's story was about a man of modest means who had run into a spell of bad luck. He lost his job and his family left him. His loss of income led to significant financial problems, so he lost his house and was, indeed, destitute. He lived on the streets, panhandling for his existence. He'd do odd jobs now and then, when he could get them, but he was just barely scraping by. He lived like this for several years.

One day late in the fall, the man sat on a park bench, anticipating his future. Winter was just around the corner, the absolute worst time of the year for the homeless. Many cold nights he could not find shelter. Fewer people were out on the streets during the winter, which meant there wouldn't be as many folks to provide him with a dollar or two from panhandling. Every winter he became terribly sick and debilitated. He was not sure he could bear another such season. He sat on that bench and contemplated his life, wondering whether or not it would be better for him to simply end it. And then he decided to pray.

He asked God for help and vowed that if God would help him, he would be the very best person he could be, always giving generously back to the Lord in thanks for his good fortune. Later that very day, a couple walking through the park noticed him. A compassionate pair, they invited him home for dinner. During their conversation they learned that the man had financial skills. It turned out that this host needed financial help in his company, so he hired the homeless man on the spot and also found him a place to live.

The homeless man excelled in the company, and, although he started out with a "meager" salary of $20,000, he remembered his vow to the Lord and gave 20 percent of his first year's income to his church. It wasn't long until he was making $50,000, and he continued to give 20 percent back to the Lord. His good fortune continued and he was able to move into a home and buy a car. He even purchased a little vacation property. The year he made $100,000, he started thinking that maybe 20 percent of $100,000 was too much to give to his church. Maybe this year he'd give just 10 percent—still a lot of money—a very generous contribution. After all, he had a lot of expenses now, and he could use some extra money to pay for them.

The formerly homeless man ultimately ended up buying the company, and his salary edged up past $500,000, and then up to $1 million a year. By this time, though, he had all sorts of financial obligations, so he decided that 2 percent was enough for the church. That still was a $20,000 contribution—equal to what he'd made during his first year with the company. Well, that year his business failed and he once again lost everything. As he walked out of the courthouse from his foreclosure proceedings, he heard a voice from the sky say, "Now that you have nothing, it will be far easier to give your fair share."

THE LESSON

The man in the story learned it was far easier to give more of his income when he had less income from which to give. Once his income became extravagant, he found it difficult to continue to give as generously. Unfortunately, that doesn't occur just in stories; it's a fact that people with modest income often give a greater percentage of it to charity than those with larger incomes.

Between 2006 and 2012, Americans who earned more than $200,000 a year reduced their charitable giving by 4.6 percent, while those earning less than $100,000 increased their giving by 4.5 percent, according to the Chronicle of Philanthropy.[3] The study based its findings on tax returns on which people itemized deductions, including charitable giving. The increase in giving among people earning less than $100,000 was despite the fact that salaries for that group had actually dropped in those six years, with a widening income gap between the rich class and the middle and poor classes.

While one can argue that the man in the story contributed only $4,000 when he gave 20 percent of his $20,000 salary and $20,000 when he gave 2 percent of his $1 million salary, the point is that he had the potential to give much more but chose not to.

I believe the percentage of what you give is important because it speaks to sacrifice. When those of modest income tithe—give 10 percent of their income to charity—it involves sacrifice. They give something up for the sake of others. They adjust their lifestyles so others can benefit. For those who make a six-figure income, however, their contributions may not impact their daily lives. That was the message of the sermon. Being successful requires you to give back, not just of your financial resources in the form of philanthropy, but also of your time and talent. Our not-for-profit and volunteer organizations are only as good as the community leaders who get involved in them. Maybe Albert Schweitzer said it best: "In gratitude for your good fortune, you must remember in return some sacrifice of your own life for another life."

---

3 *https://philanthropy.com/article/As-Wealthy-Give-Smaller-Share/152481*

Giving should not occur from a sense of obligation or because it's expected because of your stature in your company and the community. Giving should occur because it feels good. An old adage says, "Give until it hurts." I've always felt this puts a negative connotation on charity work. You should do charity work because it feels *good*, and, yes, it is the right thing to do. Making a gift that hurts is not enjoyable. Making a gift that feels good gives you a great deal of satisfaction. Attending a not-for-profit board meeting out of obligation is not nearly as enjoyable as attending this board meeting because you feel like you have something to offer and want to make a difference. Making a contribution because it's expected doesn't provide nearly the satisfaction as one you know will have an impact on a child or an elderly person in need. So find a cause you believe in and give consistently.

America is the most philanthropic country in the world. Truly, philanthropy is an American institution and a value that for many of us is passed down through our families. Families who believe in philanthropy tend to teach their children to give . . . generously. Help your children learn the value of contributing by having them give a portion of their own money to a cause of their choosing. When they feel good about that, you can be assured they'll continue to contribute throughout their lives as they are able.

When I entered the not-for-profit world, I was sometimes amazed at the number of wealthy individuals who made very modest gifts while thinking they were being generous. Over time, I learned that these people had never been taught philanthropy, and I realized that all of us need to do a better job in teaching the value of "giving until it feels good."

Philanthropy—money—is what makes it possible for not-for-profit organizations to provide more and better care. If an organization is effective at fund-raising, I challenge it to raise even more money. And if the organization has never raised money or does not do it well, I suggest that it learn proper fund-raising techniques so it can be more effective. The difference between great not-for-profit organizations and the rest often is their ability to raise money.

If you are a not-for-profit executive reading this book, I challenge you to review your fund-raising strategies. If you're raising a good deal already through philanthropy—remember that good isn't good enough—determine how you can raise more. If you're raising a modest amount or no money, bring in a fund-raising consultant and put your board on the train that is headed toward increasing the role of philanthropy at your organization.

In every organization with which I've been involved, I have established philanthropy as a primary initiative, and the initiatives have all been successful. The additional resources make it possible to improve buildings, train staff, and dramatically improve the quality of care. Caron continues its commitment to charity care by offering approximately $17 million in treatment scholarships every year. We are extremely proud of this, which would never have been possible without philanthropy!

Improving quality of care attracts even more philanthropy and generates positive momentum. Individuals want to contribute to success. They want to invest their philanthropic dollars in winning causes that make a difference in society.

If you're a not-for-profit executive, make sure to help your constituency understand the value of giving until it feels good. If you're a leader in the for-profit sector, get involved with some not-for-profits in your community, because giving back is part of the price of success. It also is a badge of honor, as a level of prestige comes with being elected and serving on important boards in your community. Select those boards on which you can truly make a difference and you have a level of passion for. But don't get involved with so many boards that you can't serve effectively on any of them. Take on only as much responsibility as you can adequately handle.

As a not-for-profit executive who continues to ask busy people to serve on boards, I greatly respect those who tell me they simply don't have the time. Pick your boards carefully, learn about the organization, understand how you can impact it, and serve responsibly. Once you're seated on the board, read the information you receive. Go to meetings with good questions and good suggestions. Understand the difference between governance and management. Let staff know that you're a resource whenever they need you. Challenge the board to continue to increase their fund-raising capabilities, and be a leader in helping them understand the value of giving until it feels good!

Chapter 29

Preserve the Mother Lode

We told a story on the farm to help us all realize what our line of work was: we were pork farmers. The story went like this. We were visiting our neighbors, and as we were sitting around outside waiting for dinner to be served, a three-legged pig walked into our midst. My father asked our neighbor why the pig had only three legs.

The neighbor responded, "Oh that's our prize pig. We're so proud of him and we owe so much to him. Remember last year when our house was being robbed? Well, this pig escaped from the pen, tackled the robber, and held him at bay until we came home and delivered a call to the county sheriff to have the robber apprehended."

"Did he break a leg or did he get hurt in the skirmish?" my father said.

"Oh no, that's not what happened," the neighbor said.

"Well, what happened to his leg?" my father asked.

"Remember the time several months ago when we had a fire in the barn? This pig helped all of our other livestock get out so that we wouldn't lose them."

"But did he break a leg in that altercation?" my father asked.

"Well, no, that's not how he lost his leg."

Finally my father said, "Please, I understand this is a great pig and he's done a lot of things for you, but how did he lose his leg?"

"Well, this pig has been so helpful to the family, and we love him so much, that we just felt that we could not eat him all at one time!"

THE LESSON

This is a crude story but one that, as farmers, we needed always to understand—that we were pork farmers and that's how we made our living. So whatever profession or walk of life you are in, remember what is most important: if you don't take care of yourself, you won't accomplish anything.

When you're working hard to establish and build a career, it's easy to forget about yourself or neglect what is important to you. I've seen many very successful people pay a high price for that success in the form of failed marriages, distant relationships with children, tough health consequences, and so forth. In Chapter 4, you prioritized values relating to your work. If family is on your list, devise a plan on how you will find balance in that area. Not finding quality time with your family will cause your relationships to suffer.

That's not to say, however, that every successful person suffers problems with their personal lives. I know many extremely successful people who have wonderful and fulfilled personal lives. The ingredient they share is that they employ the same type of planning and determination in their personal lives as they do in their careers.

For me, a meaningful family life has always been very high on my values list. My four children are grown now, but a priority for me when they were younger was to spend time together. They understood that I needed to travel often and that I frequently had to do some work in the evening, but we held sacred some traditions and activities, and they were high priorities for me.

Maybe the most important message is this: whatever time you have with family, make it quality time. Show up when you say you will, and engage with family members. Put away the phone for a while and close the laptop or tablet. Pay attention to what they're saying. Ask questions and stay on top of what's happening in their lives.

We also made it a point to have dinner as a family whenever I was at home, and, whenever possible, I set aside weekends to spend exclusively with my family. Be assured, it wasn't perfect. I missed some of their activities I would have loved to attend, but I showed up when I said I would and I engaged. That has made a huge difference.

Taking care of yourself and your family is a win-win situation for both your personal life and your work life. When your family is cared for and happy, they'll also be supportive of you and your career, and that makes it far easier to meet the demands of work. I've known individuals whose families were resentful of their careers, which made it extremely difficult for everyone. Work on your family and personal life with the same level of dedication you work on your career.

Taking time for yourself is equally as important. I've known individuals who are pretty good at business and family but become very resentful because they don't do anything for themselves. They find that the demands of increasing success and raising a family mean fewer opportunities to take part in activities they really enjoy, and, on some level, they resent both the job and their family. I believe you can be good at family and work only if you are happy about your life.

I make it a priority to take care of myself. I love to golf and do so year-round. I run every other day regardless of where I am or what I'm doing. Staying fit and healthy makes it easier for me to concentrate. It reduces stress, prevents me from becoming sick, and simply makes me feel better about myself. Whatever you enjoy doing, find the time to do it, but not at the expense of your time with your family. It's a balancing act, but it can be done.

I also encourage you to engage in some type of ongoing personal growth and learning. Seminars or webinars, inspirational books, travel, art or music lessons, online classes, and other methods are good tools for keeping fresh and excited about your work and life in general. It's fun to try and explore new experiences and places, or to master a new skill. Maintaining the mother lode—that is, yourself—takes work, but is well worth the effort.

Finally, regardless of religious orientation or background, it's important to take care of your spiritual well-being. Too often, as we become busy with careers, participation in religious activities falls off and our spiritual development is put on hold. That's too bad, because it may be during that period when a strong spiritual connection is needed the most. Developing a level of spirituality, whether it's through attending a religious community, studying philosophy, meditating, or another technique, will help sustain you in tough times and make good times even better. A person who is spiritual and has a relationship with a higher power becomes much more compassionate, is more authentic, and possesses the type of values that are critical in being truly successful.

The value in taking care of yourself is enormous, because if you don't, all of your accomplishments can come crashing down at a very high price. Stress-related health problems, marital problems, lack of inner peace, high levels of frustration, and other problems will make it very difficult for you to work at your best and achieve your maximum potential. So remember: take care of yourself, and the other pieces will fall into place.

Sometimes, in spite of your best intentions, plans, and commitment to protect the mother lode, you will encounter circumstances beyond your control. They could be related to financial hardship, divorce, illness, or other unexpected challenges. In my case it was an illness. The irony of my illness is that it was alcoholism. Given my extensive experience in the field of addiction, I was well aware that my alcohol consumption had surpassed social drinking and was actively becoming a problem. In spite of willpower, the knowledge

I had about the disease, and my external appearance that everything was okay, the disease began to control my life. I prayed to God to remove this burden or provide me with insight on how best to address it. I was continually haunted by the question of how someone in my professional position could seek help in a safe way. In the end, I was arrested for a DUI in which, thankfully, no one was hurt. I considered that event the "divine intervention," which led me to treatment in March 2008. I am grateful I had an opportunity to experience firsthand that addiction treatment works, and that life in recovery is, indeed, a blessing. I now have an even more profound connection to recovery and my chosen career. I am grateful that the Caron board of trustees, our employees, and our alumni and supporters stood by me as I embarked on this journey. More important, I am grateful that my wife and four children also supported me and embraced my recovery.

Now that I am in recovery, preserving the mother lode by also leading a life in active recovery is even more vital. Even with best intentions, we all must be ready to adjust our plans when we face forces beyond our control. Readjusting the plan, as I did, could make it better and more effective.

Part 5

WHAT NOW? ON TO THE NEXT LEVEL

As farm kids, it was routine for us to work for neighbors. As you have seen from a variety of stories throughout the book, there are all types of jobs that we could do: cutting weeds out of beans, bailing hay, driving tractors and more.

One summer, my dad suggested to me that it was time to step up to a new job—detasseling corn. I was aware of the process, which involved pulling the tassel off the top of a corn plant so that the plant could not pollinate itself. Instead, we wanted the plant to be pollinated by a different stalk of corn in order to create a hybrid that would be utilized for seed.

This job meant I'd be working for a large, hybrid seed company with people I probably didn't know, and having a regimented start and stop time. I was very nervous about it because I wondered whether I was up to the task.

After three years as a detassler, my dad suggested that since I was sixteen—and could now drive—I should apply for a supervisor role directly with the seed corn company. If I got the job, I would have to recruit my own detasslers, and I would be responsible for following the instructions and specifications of the seed corn company.

Once again, the thought of taking on new responsibility made me nervous, but with the encouragement and support of my father I applied for and got the job, and undertook the challenge for the next two years. Not only did I oversee my own crew, but I discovered there were several other advantages to this position. I learned how to work for a large organization, took on more responsibility, became a supervisor, and developed an accountable teenage work crew. I was paid considerably more for this level of work. The lesson I truly learned was that with more responsibility, accountability, and accomplishment, also comes gratification and additional rewards.

Lesson

You also may find yourself experiencing trepidation as you move into a leadership role. It's perfectly natural to have this type of emotional reaction as your career evolves. However, I hope you will use the many suggestions from this book including having a mentor (to some degree my dad was my mentor in helping me with my role). Over time, you will become comfortable in a leadership position and you will also reap the rewards of your success. Part 5 is all about that next step.

Chapter 30

The Spoils of Victory

My father owned 300 acres of land but was always looking to rent property from other farmers. This was common,
and there were a couple of ways to do it. Some farmers
rented land on other farms simply by paying a fee. My dad,
however, preferred to rent by sharing the costs of planting,
cultivating, and harvesting the crop, and then sharing the
proceeds the crops generated. In a bad year, the owner of the
land and my father would suffer equally. In a good year, they
were equally successful. He believed that when the land-
owner and the renter had an equal investment, they would
cooperate in order to yield the best results, making decisions
that would be equally beneficial. If only one person bore the
risk, it would be easy for the other to be less committed to
assuring the success of the venture.

As you become increasingly successful, you typically will
undertake ventures that involve greater risk than you've

previously encountered. Beefing up your performance by taking on greater risk can significantly increase your outcomes and enable you to reap the rewards of a successful crop.

The Lesson

To the victor go the spoils. Traditionally, when one army is victorious over another, conquering soldiers help themselves to the other army's livestock, palace jewels, grain from the farms, or whatever else they want. Clearly, they benefit from a successful military endeavor.

It's not all that much different in business, except our equivalent is the bonus system. Not all companies offer these programs. Some companies discontinued or limited them after the economic downturn of 2008. However, at Caron, we find that bonuses continue to be valuable tools for our organization and motivation for the staff. Incentive or bonus compensation, which is additional pay for employees who perform beyond moderate expectations, is a tangible reward and recognition for people who achieve high levels of success. Many employees respond favorably to these types of programs. (The bonus is generated by the company's "better than expected" performance. This additional income is then distributed in a predetermined and approved manner to employees for their role in generating the surplus.)

If your company has a similar program, I encourage you to take full advantage of it. I challenge you to put more of your salary at risk, which means you would have a smaller salary but opportunity for a greater bonus when you succeed. By doing so, you indicate that you are confident in your ability to succeed and willing to take some risk for greater rewards. If your organization does not have a compensation-based incentive program and you are in a position to impact that, I recommend you do so. Perhaps you could lobby to have a pilot program within your department. If you're successful, it will be well worth your energy. Consult with a compensation expert to develop a plan.

I have used incentive-based compensation for my staff and myself for many years at Caron. I found it particularly beneficial when I became president in 1995. The organization, for various reasons, had been struggling financially for some time before I arrived. In my first year we developed a plan for the employee pension and bonus plan. Once the organization hit a certain level of financial success, the plan "triggered" and rewarded all levels of employees based on corporate performance first and then individual performance. It's been a fabulous program, and the financial performance of the organization has reached all-time high levels while providing pension and bonus compensation for employees who exceeded expectations.

At the senior level, the plan has been extremely valuable in attracting and retaining important talent. The beauty of the program is that everyone in the organization becomes aware of what they can do to impact the financial performance of the organization. This includes cutting back on expenses and coming up with cost-cutting ideas that still yield a return on investment. Employee morale is typically higher when they will benefit as a result of their efforts.

If you are already at a senior level within your organization, demonstrate your faith in your abilities by striving toward making higher levels of bonuses available, both on an annual and a strategic-plan cycle basis (whatever that might be, three to five years). I have found that this leads to greater levels of compensation, and it clearly demonstrates to your superiors your confidence in your ability to perform. It's part of the "aiming for the moon and then delivering" concept we discussed in Chapter 10.

Leveraging part of your salary against an incentive compensation plan becomes an excellent bargaining tool for more compensation, as many times organizations have concerns about the size of raises, or they want to keep salaries within certain limits. Superiors, however, can often be convinced to go along with an incentive compensation proposal because it pays out only if the resources are available. Those resources, of course, are a direct result of your performance. Just make sure you heed good advice and careful detail when developing this type of plan. Include as many employees within the organization as possible in this program. By helping them be successful, they will help you be successful.

Chapter 31

Raise the Bar

Missouri is a border state, meaning that some residents consider themselves Northerners, while others consider themselves Southerners. There's a story about a political rally at which the speaker was of Southern descent. Someone who considered himself a Northerner stood up and said, "I was born a Yankee, I was raised a Yankee, and I intend to die a Yankee."

The Southerner replied, "Not very high expectations, eh?"

THE LESSON

Chapter 24, Good Ain't Good Enough Anymore, discussed the importance of ongoing employee and organizational development. While some of the same information is contained here, this chapter focuses on you. As you achieve success, it's imperative that you continue to evaluate your five-year plan. Once you've reached the hundred-foot target we began working on back in Chapter 2, don't rest on your laurels but keep pushing your game and working to improve.

Life is an ongoing series of changes, and you need to keep up with them. Since circumstances change, you need to as well. When you reach a senior level, it's probably time to assess whether you have the right mentors. It could be that you've surpassed your mentors and need to seek out a professional who is at a higher level. If you need a new mentor or mentors, utilize the same process you did previously, but select people who will challenge you even more. Review your five-year plan and long-term vision to determine whether it is proactive and aggressive enough for you at your current level of success. Remember, you are a different person today from when you first developed those plans. You may be aiming for higher levels of success. As you reassess your business-related values, you may do some shifting around. For example, convenience, stability, and a family friendly environment may be more important to you now. A few chapters back I recommended that you complete a 360-degree review process to determine your perceived strengths and weaknesses. The real benefit of this type of review is that it's not only an assessment of how you are doing but it's also a tool for facilitating a plan to help you overcome shortcomings, accentuate your strengths, and develop strategies for dealing with your colleagues. The 360-degree review is a terrific tool when you're trying to raise the bar.

My goal at age sixteen was to enter seminary and become a minister. Obviously, my plans have taken me down a different path, and I may never become a preacher. As I grow older, I see some of my values regarding work changing as well. As you raise the bar, it doesn't have to be for increased power, more financial reward, additional authority, or added prestige. Raising the bar means that you continue to challenge yourself and ask yourself what you really want to do and accomplish. You should never stop planning and working your plan if you want to set and achieve goals throughout your lifetime. When you raise the bar on yourself, you will continue to experience the gratification that comes with having a clear idea of where you want to go and the satisfaction when you get there. While I never became a minister, I do believe I have "done the Lord's work" in many other ways. I've continued to raise my bar on what that means to me, and the satisfaction and gratification is rewarding.

Chapter 32

How Would You Beat Yourself?

Two old farmers were extremely competitive. They were always looking for ways to one-up the other. One day they went hunting together, and one of the farmers couldn't wait to show up the other with a new trick he'd taught his dog. The farmer had taught his dog to walk on water, something he was positive would greatly impress his neighbor.

The neighbor shot a duck, and the farmer's dog walked out on top of the water, picked up the bird, and brought it back. The neighbor said nothing, not even acknowledging what the dog had done. This went on all day. Every time one of the old farmers shot a duck, the dog walked out on the water and brought the duck back, never once splashing the men.

By the end of the day, the first farmer couldn't stand it anymore. He said to his neighbor, "Have you even noticed what my dog has been doing all day?"

The second farmer replied, "Oh yes, I noticed, but I was too embarrassed to say anything about the fact that your dog can't swim!"

THE LESSON

While trying to one-up his neighbor, the old farmer became frustrated when he didn't achieve his desired results. It would have been healthier if he focused on being proud of his dog rather than using the dog's accomplishment to impress his neighbor. As you work to improve yourself, make sure the improvements are for the betterment of you—not an attempt to be better than everyone else.

I added this concept just recently when I heard the chairman of a Fortune 1000 company tell me that he took his senior executives away annually for a day of retreat and spent the day brainstorming as if they had unlimited resources. What would they do to "beat" their current company? What would they do to take away market share? What would they do to steal important personnel? What would they do in the area of research or development to come up with a better product? What would they do to improve or provide superior customer service? This exercise always provided excellent strategies. They say the best defense for such a situation could be a good offense. So the company always came up with ideas to implement, which kept them way ahead of the competition.

I believe that you should do the same thing as you look at your plan, your progress, and your results. Look at those areas of your plan, your career, and identify where you are the weakest. For example, do you have as good a mentor as you should? Are you crystal clear on your values? Is your current job consistent with your plan? Are you receiving the compensation you want? Take an occasional hard look at everything and make sure you are, indeed, on a solid foundation. As you look at your career, plan, values, etc., and identify areas where you are beatable, include a plan for improvement in those areas.

Maybe as you go through your values, you realize that your family life is not what you would like it to be. Perhaps as you look at taking care of yourself, you learn that you don't have the type of spiritual development you would like. Possibly, as you look at your motivation of staff, you're not as authentic as you would like. Maybe as you consider how you communicate, you discover that your skills are not as solid as they need to be. Regardless of who we are, we *all* have areas of weaknesses. So it is important to take careful inventory periodically and develop strategies for improving those areas. No one likes to be beaten. You can help prevent that from happening by developing a strategy to beat yourself. You have to be one step ahead of the game so your professional skills and value don't become obsolete.

Let's look at the analogy to a video store, for example. At one time, going to the video store was the standard practice for renting a movie. But technology has eliminated the need for that. Likewise, after having taken an honest and searching inventory of your weaknesses, begin working on those skills so that you are truly unbeatable.

Chapter 33

Freely Giving What Has Been Given to You

One bright Saturday morning, a boy bounded down the steps to breakfast. His mother commented that he seemed very excited and asked him what he had planned for the day.

"I'm going out on a trip of great discovery."

When his mother asked what he hoped to discover, he said, "I'm going to find God today."

This amused the mother. She wished her son luck for his trip, told him to go no farther than the park across the street, and packed some treats for him in his backpack.

The boy went to the park and began exploring, but soon he became thirsty and started thinking about the juice bottles he'd seen his mom pack. He found a bench, sat down, and rummaged through his backpack for the juice. An elderly woman sat down at the other end of the bench and smiled at him. He smiled back as he grabbed one of the bottles and opened it. After taking a few sips, he realized it would be a good thing to ask his bench mate if she wanted the other bottle of juice. He offered it to her and she graciously accepted, giving him another kind smile.

After he drank the juice, he played on the swing set and other playground equipment, but then he became hungry, so he returned to the bench, where the elderly woman was keeping an eye on his backpack. The boy dug through it and pulled out the cookies his mom had packed. Again, he thought to offer one to the woman, and again she graciously accepted with a friendly smile and a nod.

When he finished the cookies, the boy decided to go home. He said good-bye to his new friend and started walking away. Quickly, he turned around, came back to the elderly woman, and gave her a big hug. She said good-bye with the biggest and kindest smile he had ever seen.

When he went home, his mother asked, "How was your trip? Did you find God?"

"Yes, I did," the boy replied, "and she has the prettiest smile I've ever seen."

Meanwhile, in a different neighborhood, the elderly woman's son stopped in to visit her. He noticed that his mother seemed very upbeat and content, so he asked her why. She responded that she had seen God that day. "And he was much younger than I expected."

God works through people, and many of them have probably crossed your path. You will no doubt have help in achieving your goals and becoming successful in business. It is important to allow God to work through you to help others. Taking this step keeps the cycle of people helping people moving forward.

THE LESSON

You have become successful but not completely on your own. You developed and worked your plan, but you had help from mentors, supervisors, and staff. Once you've achieved success, you have an obligation to share the keys of success with others. One way you can do that is to offer to mentor a bright and talented young person, either within your company or outside.

If you choose someone within your company, consider it a temporary situation. If you think back to Chapter 4, You Can't Count Your Cows if You Don't Know Where They Are, you might recall that it's preferable to have a mentor who does not work in the same place, because an outside person can be more objective and others may see this as preferential treatment. You could, however, offer to act as mentor until the younger employee finds someone outside of the company. You can work with the employee and share the keys to success, teaching him or her how to identify and rate values, develop a plan, act like a boss, and be successful. If the employee is a member of your organization, this relationship could help to move the company ahead as well as provide a valuable service for the mentee.

Another reason to serve as a mentor is that by sharing your skills and strategies for success, you force yourself to continue to utilize them. I've learned in the addiction treatment field that individuals who continue to teach others about recovery enhance their own recoveries. The same is true with mentoring. As you teach, you reinforce your good habits and behaviors and strategies for yourself. You can't mentor someone on the value of a five-year plan if you don't have one yourself. You can't ask others to prioritize their values if you haven't done so. You can't encourage other people to have a balanced life and take care of themselves if you don't. Teaching others about these strategies serves as a consistent reminder of how to be successful.

Building a helping relationship with another person also has the potential benefit of an ongoing and lifelong friendship. It's extremely gratifying to watch as someone you have helped becomes successful. Just as you have a great sense of loyalty and friendship toward those who have helped you along in your career, that loyalty and friendship will return to you. These genuine friendships, built on blood, sweat, and tears, are meaningful and priceless. A final step toward success is to give what you have received. You'll find that giving it away is, indeed, the best way to keep it.

Part 6

CONCLUSION

The events of my eighth birthday far exceeded what I had anticipated. Most years, after looking forward to my birthday for weeks and weeks, the actual birthday was a little bit of a letdown. Not this one, however.

What I asked for on my eighth birthday was to be able to plow the pastures, which meant driving a tractor that pulled a plow and turned over the soil. I had toy tractors of my own and had ridden on the tractor with my dad and grandfather as they plowed, but I longed for the day when I could do it myself. I wanted to feel the power of the tractor and to look behind me and see whatever it was I was plowing yield to fresh, black, and fertile soil.

So on the day of my birthday, my dad put me on a small Ford tractor that pulled a small plow with two fourteen-inch blades. At the time, I didn't realize that this particular tractor had very little power, or that my mother was not in favor of this whole idea. I was absolutely thrilled at the thought of plowing a field.

Off we went, my father showing me the safety features of the equipment. He said that we would drive to the middle of the field, and then I would drive in a straight line from one side to the other. I told him I was sure I could do that. I sat on the tractor with the plow on the ground behind me, my arms rigid and holding the wheel perfectly straight, and drove to the other side of the field. I hadn't looked back once, sitting perfectly still for the entire quarter mile. My dad asked me how I thought I'd done, and I told him I thought the path I drove would be as straight as an arrow. When I turned around to look at the nice, straight line I'd plowed, I was shocked. I saw a curvy, wavy line—not straight in the least! I was disappointed and asked my father how that could have happened. I thought I had kept the tractor perfectly straight.

He explained that the problem with this tractor, like most tractors, is that there is a great deal of play in the steering wheel. If the tractor didn't go perfectly straight, it's because you're holding the steering wheel straight and the wheels move around with the nuances of the ground and unevenness of the terrain. I asked him what the trick was to plowing in a straight line. My dad told me that it's easy: you simply pick out a post, a telephone pole, or a tree at the other side of the field, and drive straight toward it.

We turned the tractor around and I picked out a telephone pole on the other side of the field. The steering wheel was moving all over the place, and my arms were bouncing around, but when I drove to the other side of the field and looked back, I saw that I had plowed a straight line.

THE LESSON

Setting your sights on a goal and heading straight for it doesn't apply only to plowing a field or mowing grass; it's what we need to do in life. Pick a point or a goal for the future and stay focused on that. Your wheels may turn a little, and your arms will bounce a bit, and some situations won't go exactly as planned, but you'll be on a fairly straight line toward your target if you stay focused. You don't want to lock yourself on to a path, because you might find it's not the right one and you'll need to make a change. But picking a goal and staying focused on it should keep you on a straight course.

Helping you to focus on the target or goal so that you move forward in a direct line is the purpose of this book. Unfortunately, it's not as easy as plowing a straight line, because you'll have distractions and life throws us curveballs. You'll start and not always follow through, and you'll need to be reminded of what to do next to keep moving toward your goal.

You've read nearly this entire book now, and I hope you've taken many lessons from it and have participated in the exercises. I hope you'll continue to refer to different parts of the book as you need them. As you read through the chapter that follows, you'll find a summary of the important tools and exercises you read about earlier. Following the conclusion is a handy reference and overview of all of the tools mentioned. I hope that as you begin to use these tools, you'll find them as effective as focusing on a target to plow a straight line.

Chapter 34

What Not to Forget

When I was a kid, we sometimes traveled by train. My father told us to keep our tickets in a safe place where we could easily find them when the conductor came around. He told us a story about train tickets involving Chief Justice Oliver Wendell Holmes, a Civil War veteran who served as a Supreme Court Justice from 1902 to 1932.

The chief justice was traveling on a train and noticed that a porter was coming to take his ticket. He fumbled around looking for it but couldn't find it. Recognizing the distinguished gentleman, the porter told him it was no problem that he couldn't find his ticket. "If you come across it, mail it to the railroad company and all will be well."

The chief justice told the porter that while he appreciated the consideration, the missing ticket was, indeed, a problem. "I can't remember my destination and need the ticket to tell me where I'm going!"

THE LESSON

If you're not sure where you're going, it's easy to forget how to get there. Let's review the most important lessons, themes, and tools contained in this book.

How to Achieve Success

1. **Take responsibility** for your situation or circumstances. You have the power to change the circumstances you don't like and to build on those you do. Regardless of your background or upbringing, be accountable and move forward.

2. **Ask for help** when you need it. Find a mentor or mentors. Learn from good bosses. Observe others and pay attention to their styles and how they navigate. And remember, studying never hurts.

3. **Work hard** to develop a five-year plan, and continue to work that plan. Frequently assess your progress and continue to update it. Use the other tools contained in this book, as well.

The result: **you will receive far more than you bargained for.** By effectively working these three steps, you will be prepared to move ahead. Remember that when you've achieved more than you bargained for, you'll need to give until it feels good, give freely what has been given to you, and pay attention to taking care of yourself and others. Give it to keep it.

Top Leadership Lessons

1. **Want to be a leader.** It doesn't matter what type of unique ability you have or what type of training you have received. To succeed, you have to desire to be a leader.

2. **Plan to be a leader.** Instead of wishing or hoping you'll be a leader, plan on becoming a leader. Develop and work a plan that continues to move you along the path to where you want to be.

3. **Act like a leader.** Don't start acting like a leader when you finally arrive at the "Promised Land"; start acting like one long before. Acting like a leader in advance of when you are one will let others know that you possess the qualities and characteristics necessary to be one.

4. **Be successful.** Do more than you need to, always going the extra mile. By doing so, you'll gain a reputation as a reliable and successful person. Success builds on success, so use the tools contained in this book to help you establish yourself as a successful person.

5. **Move on to the next level of achievement.** There is always more to do and room for improvement. Be sure to give back so that you'll never forget what you have learned.

The Themes of Achievement

1. **Mission.** Your mission is the end result of your five-year plan. This is the collective result of successfully achieving your job-related values, such as the position, salary, prestige, and whatever else is important to you. Be clear about what you hope to achieve. Without a mission or a clear goal, it is impossible to become truly successful.

2. **Values.** They define who you are, what you hold true, and how you go about doing your work. Make sure they reflect you and are authentic. The values by which you define yourself should be the same that others use to define you.

3. **Passion.** Pursue all tasks with gusto and enthusiasm. This signals to others that you truly care about what you do.

4. **Vision.** Conceptualize your ultimate goal, your own moon landing. Where do you want to be? As you work through your series of five-year plans, this is what you are eventually hoping to achieve.

5. **Staff.** You can't accomplish all of these important goals alone. A general without soldiers doesn't have an army. A good leader has an effective team. Pay particular attention to the tools that outline how to motivate and take care of your employees. A healthy and productive staff will always make you look good.

Top Seven Tools for Reaching Your Career Goals

1. The ten job-related values and how to prioritize them. (Appendix D)

2. The five-year plan: what to include in it, how to develop it, and how to utilize it. (Appendix G)

3. The mentoring program: how to select and utilize an effective mentor. (Appendix F)

4. How to develop your style: what values do you want people to use to describe you? (Appendix E)

5. Your boss and the grid: which one of the four quadrants does your boss fall into? Develop a strategy for learning from them based on the quadrant. (Appendix J)

6. How to interview and be interviewed: avoid the most common critical mistakes and go in with good questions.

7. Decision charting: make sure you know who has the V and follow up every meeting with action items, even if it's a meeting with only two people. (Appendix H)

You'll also want to refer to the other information and tests contained in the appendices, along with references to books, articles, and resources for not-for-profits. The most important point I hope you'll take with you from this book, however, is the lesson of the chicken story I shared in the Introduction: take responsibility, ask for help, and work hard to achieve more than you bargained for.

If you take those actions, you will, indeed, have the potential to become a boss who is a true leader and for whom employees aspire to work. When you reach that level, you'll receive far more than you bargained for not just in the workplace but in all aspects of your life.

Good luck, boss!

APPENDICES

APPENDIX A:
The Steps to Being a Leader

STEP 1: **Want to Be**

STEP 2: **Plan to Be**

STEP 3: **Act Like It**

STEP 4: **Be Successful**

STEP 5: **On to the Next Level**

STEP 6: **What Not to Forget**

APPENDIX B:
Twenty Characteristics of Leaders

Authors James Kouzes and Barry Posner identify twenty characteristics of leaders in their "Leadership Challenge" (*Credibility*, published in 2003 by Jossey-Bass). Kouzes and Posner have periodically conducted this survey since 1989. Four leadership characteristics are consistently ranked highest over the years: honesty, forward-looking, inspiring, and competent.

1. Honesty
2. Forward-looking
3. Inspiring
4. Competent
5. Fair-minded
6. Supportive
7. Broad-minded
8. Intelligent
9. Straightforward
10. Courageous
11. Dependable
12. Cooperative
13. Imaginative
14. Caring
15. Mature
16. Determined
17. Ambitious
18. Loyal
19. Self-controlled
20. Independent

APPENDIX C: Leadership, Learning, and Interest Tests

The following list is not intended to be a complete list; rather it provides a sample of commonly used, effective tools. Any corporate psychologist can provide guidance in this area.

+ Myers-Briggs
+ Caliper
+ Occupational Personality Questionnaire (OPQ 32)
+ LSI (Life Styles Inventory)
+ 360-Degree Review

APPENDIX D:
Ten Job-Related Values

During a time of low stress, prioritize the following values from 1 to 10, with 1 being the most important and 10 being the least. Then give each a percentage of how important so that the total adds up to 100 percent. For example, if you choose family, convenience, comfort, need to make a difference, and interesting, you might decide to apply 40 percent to family, and then 15 percent to each additional value for a total of 100 percent.

The Values: How Important Are Each to You?

Financial

1	2	3	4	5	6	7	8	9	10

Comfort / Lack of stress

1	2	3	4	5	6	7	8	9	10

Power / Influence

1	2	3	4	5	6	7	8	9	10

Convenience

1	2	3	4	5	6	7	8	9	10

Family Impact

1   2   3   4   5   6   7   8   9   10

Your Need to Serve / Make a Difference

1   2   3   4   5   6   7   8   9   10

Visibility / Prestige

1   2   3   4   5   6   7   8   9   10

Entrepreneurship

1   2   3   4   5   6   7   8   9   10

Challenge

1   2   3   4   5   6   7   8   9   10

Interesting / Fun

1   2   3   4   5   6   7   8   9   10

C:/homeonexchange/NAATPConf.Presentation/10PersonalJobRelatedValues

APPENDIX E:
Value/Style Development

1. Observations about other impressive leaders.

   What impresses me/what I like/what I want to "copy."

   _____

   _____

   _____

   What repulses me/what I don't like/what I want to avoid.

   _____

   _____

   _____

2. What five values do I want to be my trademark?

   Add two to the three that everyone must have:

   1. Honesty/integrity

   2. Forward-looking

   3. Inspirational

   4. _____

   5. _____

Five others to round out your style:

6. _____

7. _____

8. _____

9. _____

10. _____

3. Ask others to identify the values and style that they think describe you.

How consistent is your goal with the perception?

_____

_____

_____

C:homeonexchange/NAATPpresentation Value/styledevelopment

APPENDIX F:
Working with a Mentor

1. Candidates

_____

_____

_____

2. Recruitment Efforts

_____

_____

_____

3. Selection

_____

_____

_____

4. Meeting Dates

_____

_____

_____

5. Advice from Mentor

_____

_____

_____

6. Follow-Up with Mentor/What Have I Changed

_____

_____

_____

C:homeonexchangeNAATPpresentationMentor

APPENDIX G: Five-Year Plan

Preparing your five-year-plan may be the most important lesson from this book. Chapter 4 offers a significant explanation and foundation for this exercise. Take time to give careful consideration to where you would like your career and compensation to be five years down the road, and then provide yourself with ample time to put it down on paper. Appendix G is the framework for that plan. Good luck!

APPENDIX H: Action Plan

Chapter 13 provides a detailed overview on how to use action/decision minutes. Below is the simple form that you can utilize. This is an effective way to "take charge" of a meeting and the next steps. A brief overview would be to write the task under the description. The result of the task either needs to be a decision or an action completed. In accordance with my recommendations in the previously mentioned chapter, you would also include the deadline for each action. The decision charting is a list of individuals who have the various responsibilities, and then the notes/comments or any other further descriptions, as well as a place for a status report.

APPENDIX I:
Factors Affecting Job Attitudes

If the factors in Section A are not attained, it's very difficult for an organization to overcome even if it does all the factors well in Section B.

A. Factors characterizing events on the job that led to extreme satisfaction.

If these are done well, they will be the primary cause of job satisfaction.

1. Achievement 42%
2. Recognition 32%
3. Work Itself 23%
4. Responsibility 22%
5. Advancement 10%
6. Growth 7%

B. Factors characterizing events on the job that led to extreme dissatisfaction.

If these are not done well, they will be the primary cause of job dissatisfaction.

1. Company Policy and Administration 35%

2. Supervision 20%

3. Relationship with Supervisor 12%

4. Work Conditions 10%

5. Salary 9%

6. Relationship with Peers 8%

7. Personal Life 5%

8. Relationship with Subordinates 5%

9. Status 4%

10. Security 3%

NOTE: The figures total more than 100 percent on both A and B because often two factors can be attributed to a single event.

Source: Harvard Business Review, *September–October 1987*

APPENDIX J: Your Boss Assessment Leadership Qualities

	Plus	Plus	**Minus**
P	+ Leadership Quality		– Leadership Quality
E	+ Personality		+ Personality
R			
S		(1)	(2)
O	Plus ◄————		————► Minus
N		(3)	(4)
A			
L	+ Leadership Quality		- Leadership Quality
I	- Personality		- Personality
T			
Y		Minus	

Strategy for Each

1. Develop partnership; potential future mentor.
2. The most dangerous; very deceptive; potential "Peter Principle"; be careful.

3. Can learn a great deal if you are proactive in developing guidelines.

4. Don't get here; learn what "not to do"; exercise exit visa or stage "Palace Coup."

C:homeonexchange.NAATPconf.Presentation

RECOMMENDED READING

Books for Management

Build a Better Life by Stealing Office Supplies by Scott Adams. Kansas City, Missouri: Andrews & McMeel, 1994.

Casual Day Has Gone Too Far by Scott Adams. Kansas City, Missouri: Andrews & McMeel, 1997.

Credibility: How Leaders Gain and Lose It, Why People Demand It by James Kouzes and Barry Posner. San Francisco: Jossey-Bass, 1993.

Dogbert's Top Secret Management Handbook by Scott Adams. New York: HarperCollins Publisher, 1997.

It's Obvious You Won't Survive by Your Wits Alone by Scott Adams. Kansas City, Missouri: Andrews & McMeel, 1995.

One Minute Manager by Ken Blanchard and Spencer Johnson. New York: William Morrow & Co., 1982.

Start with Why: How Great Leaders Inspire Everyone to Take Action by Simon Sinek. London: Penguin Group, 2011.

The Dilbert Principle: A Cubicle's-Eye View of Bosses, Meetings, Management Fads & Other Workplace Afflictions by Scott Adams. New York: HarperCollins Publisher, 1996.

The Power of Noticing: What the Best Leaders See by Max Bazerman. New York: Simon & Schuster, 2014.

Who Moved My Cheese? An Amazing Way to Deal with Change in Your Work and in Your Life by Spencer Johnson. New York: Penguin Group USA, 1998.

Books for Self-Improvement

The Art of Talking So That People Will Listen by Paul Swets. New York: Simon & Schuster, 1986.

How the World Sees You: Discover Your Highest Value Through the Science of Fascination by Sally Hogshead. New York: HarperCollins Publishers, 2014.

How to Win Friends and Influence People by Dale Carnegie. New York: Simon & Schuster, 1998.

The Magic of Thinking Big by David Schwartz. New York: Simon & Schuster, 1987.

The Seven Habits of Highly Effective People by Stephen Covey. New York: Simon & Schuster, 2004.

Think and Grow Rich by Napoleon Hill. New York: Random House, 1987.

Magazine Articles

"One More Time: How Do You Motivate Employees?" by Frederick Herzberg. *Harvard Business Review*, November–December 1998.

"What Makes a Leader?" by Daniel Goleman. *Harvard Business Review*, September–October 1998.

Books for Not-for-Profit Management

Boardroom Verities by Jerold Panas. Lanham, Maryland: National Book Network, 2003.

The Board Member's Guide to Fund Raising by Fisher Howe. New York: John Wiley and Sons, 1991.

Not-for-Profit Organization

BoardSource
750 9th Street, NW, Suite 650
Washington, DC 20001-4793
Phone: (202) 349-2500 Fax: (202) 349-2599
www.boardsource.org